BLESSED BY LESS

BLESSED BY LESS

CLEARING YOUR LIFE OF CLUTTER BY LIVING LIGHTLY

SUSAN V. VOGT

LOYOLAPRESS.
A JESUIT MINISTRY
Chicago

LOYOLA PRESS.
A JESUIT MINISTRY

3441 N. Ashland Avenue
Chicago, Illinois 60657
(800) 621-1008
www.loyolapress.com

Scripture quotations contained herein are from the *New Revised Standard Version Bible: Catholic Edition*, copyright © 1993 and 1989 by the Division of Christian Education of the National Council of the Churches of Christ in the U.S.A. Used by permission. All rights reserved.

Cover art credit: ©iStockphoto.com/feoris

ISBN-13: 978-0-8294-3902-1
ISBN-10: 0-8294-3902-1
Library of Congress Control Number: 2013945009

Printed in the United States of America.

13 14 15 16 17 18 Bang 10 9 8 7 6 5 4 3 2 1

To my husband, Jim, and our four children, Brian, Heidi, Dacian, and Aaron, who allow their lives and possessions to be laid bare for the world to know. They are the ones who have to endure my crazy experiments in life like getting rid of their high school papers and sometimes mistakenly giving away a forgotten jacket.

To the Anawim Community—my local Marianist Lay Community—who share my faith and values. They experiment with me, test my ideas, hold me accountable, and give me the courage to live with less because we support and share with one another.

Contents

Preface

The Story behind the Book

My husband and I did not quickly or easily come to our desire to live more lightly. We both were fortunate to grow up in families with the ability to pay for college educations and a lot more. We are grateful for these advantages, but college also opened our eyes to the reality that many people did not have the advantages that had been normal for us. The more we observed the world around us, the more we sought a deeper spirituality. And the more we did that, the more we felt compelled to give back—or at least not take as much of the world's resources.

For decades now we have been trying to live more simply. But as time passed and our family grew, I noticed that I continued to accumulate a lot of stuff. Because I tend to be a pretty organized person, many items were neatly stored away for a rainy day—or eventually for the grandchildren I hoped to have. The grandchildren came, but their parents didn't need or want thirty-year-old outfits with spit-up stains on them. Also, I thought I could do better. The needs of my community and the Catholic faith that formed me from childhood required a renewed effort at living lightly. I started to reassess what all this saving was about.

Thus was born the decision to give away at least one thing a day for Lent. This Christian penitential season of six weeks seemed long enough to make a difference, and giving stuff away would be an appropriate sacrifice. I blogged about it (www.SusanVogt.net/blog) in order to hold myself accountable and possibly to inspire others to make their own experiments. Lent came and went, and I was becoming addicted to identifying things I no longer needed. I decided to continue the practice for a year. The ironic thing is that instead of feeling poorer, I felt freer and more fulfilled.

At the end of the year, another Lent was approaching, and again I was looking for a meaningful way to deepen my spiritual life. I came across the Food Stamp Challenge. Several lawmakers and celebrities had tried it for a week to bring awareness to the difficulty of eating nutritiously on $4.50/day—the average Food Stamp budget. My husband and I agreed to do the Food Stamp Challenge during the next six weeks of Lent. Since we are now a household of two, this meant we had $9.00/day to spend on food. We didn't starve, but it wasn't easy and we stopped when the six weeks were over. We both learned a lot about ourselves, about what food means to us, and just a little bit about what it must feel like to try to live like that all the time.

As I write this, another Lent has beckoned, and I'm trying to reduce how much stuff I put in the trash. Again I need my husband's compliance because making garbage is a joint activity.

If you picked up this book, the idea of getting along with less stuff has some appeal to you. You may not choose the activities I did, but I hope that my experiences may inspire, inform, and motivate you to assess what really gives your life meaning.

As a lifelong Catholic I certainly bring that heritage to my decisions. In my own spiritual journey I have been influenced by the Judeo-Christian Scriptures and people of faith who have gone before me. In learning about other spiritual traditions, however, I recognize that the search for God and a spiritual core is universal. I think the deeply rooted instinct to live more lightly upon this earth transcends any one religion and abides in conscientious people of good will.

Special Features of *Blessed by Less*

Connecting to Your Stage of Life focuses on the unique ways that people of different ages might apply the chapter's material to their own situations. For example:

People in the first half of life of necessity are accumulating stuff for the journey but want to keep it under control. You want to live more lightly while still being responsible adults. How?

People in the second half of life (you decide when that begins) may find this even more useful as you assess how to let go of many items accumulated over a lifetime. Some are material, some are memories or habits. It can lighten your spirit to give to others things you no longer need.

First Steps and Big Steps offers practical steps for both beginners and veterans.

Light and Easy gives tips for those just testing the waters of living more lightly. It offers an easy step for the beginner or the fainthearted.

Extreme Lightness offers a challenge to those who may have been committed to simplifying their lives for a long time and are ready to go "all in."

For Meditation offers a Scripture verse or passage to ground your journey.

For Reflection or Discussion provides engaging questions for personal reflection or group discussion.

1

Spiritual Principles for Living Lightly

When I finished college, I put all my earthly possessions in a VW beetle and moved 200 miles to Cleveland, Ohio. It did bust my car's alternator, but at that time in life I had enough. Married and four kids later, I'm a few pounds heavier and my possessions are tons heavier. Not only do I have more clothes and furniture (plus technology that hadn't been invented a generation ago), I am also storing stuff for our adult children and have all kinds of memorabilia that have accumulated over years of family life. Sometimes I feel heavier than my weight. I decided that I wanted to lighten my life by letting go of some of the stuff that crowded my house and my mind.

Your life is an overflowing closet. You know it is. There are sweatshirts folded up in a corner of your mind where your children's birthdays should be stored. That worry about the rust on the car is taking up the space that you had reserved for a slow cup of tea in the morning. I know how you feel. And guess what? There's a way to get stuff back where it belongs: let go of some of it.

Living lightly is not just about the stuff we accumulate, and it's not just for people in the second half of life. It's about an attitude of living with fewer burdens and encumbrances, whether you're twenty-one or sixty-five. When done with honest self-awareness, the journey toward living more lightly has moved me to realize that I am blessed by less. Less stuff and worries have opened space to live with more

1

contentment and meaning. Living lightly reminds me that my existence is more than accumulating possessions and status. Ultimately, I am on a spiritual pilgrimage.

As I continue to strip away the unnecessary stuff in my closets and mind, I've been able to see more clearly how much is enough and how much is more than enough. It's a delicate dance to balance my own genuine needs with those of others. The spiritual paradox is that the less tightly I cling to my stuff, my way, and my concerns, the happier and more blessed I feel. Once I have enough, less is more.

If we believe that a Divine Presence brought all of creation into being and it was good, then it follows that this God loves us unconditionally and sees our goodness despite our human failings. God's love for us is not dependent on our possessions, appearance, or accomplishments.

St. Ignatius of Loyola, who gave us the Spiritual Exercises that have been used to help people's spiritual formation for nearly five centuries, describes these attributes of a spiritually healthy and balanced life as follows:

- Detachment from the things and worries of this world.
- Spiritual freedom from all that might distract us from the ultimate purpose of our life in order to focus on what is essential—a deeper relationship with God.
- The practiced ability to find God's presence "in all things"—in our ordinary situations.

As we seek to recognize the Divine in all of life, we humans grow in the awareness that it's not all about me. We start to see more clearly what is important and what our personal false gods may be. Our human and planetary lives need many things to survive, but the more we can free ourselves from undue attachment to things that will pass away, the deeper our happiness will be. The spiritual principles that guide this book, therefore, are about letting go of what is less important to make way for a contemplative heart in action. Here are the principles:

1. My worth and importance are not dependent on *what I own*.

    - Consume less—save more money.
    - Hang on to less—become more generous, feel freer.
    - Carry less—move more lightly.

2. My worth and importance are not dependent on *how I look and feel*.

    - Eat less junk—become healthier.
    - Hurry and worry less—smile and laugh more.

3. My worth and importance are not dependent on *how much I know and what I can accomplish*.

    - TMI (Too Much Information)—choose what's important.
    - Waste less—save more time and energy.

4. Spirituality is about seeking the Divine Presence. It's not all about *me*.

    - Complain and judge less—become more at peace.
    - Control people less—love and free others.

5. God's presence surrounds me if I but look and listen. The spiritual response is to turn this contemplative awareness into action for the good of humanity.

    - Let go of cheap faith—gain a deeper faith for the long haul.

There is a time for setting up a household, and certainly as parents we are responsible to feed, clothe, and shelter our children. All this takes money and increases our possessions. Living lightly may seem out of reach to an active, growing family. But do we really need *all* the stuff that crowds our closets and basements? When it's hard to find things, the beauty of our dwelling space is marred by clutter. When we own things that we no longer need but others do need, it becomes a matter of justice. How does a conscientious person discern how much is enough and why less is better? Everyone's level of "less" is different.

How Is Less Better?

Why would anyone want to have less than they could afford? Some basics—food, clothing, shelter, education, health care, and safety—are necessary. Many more things such as furniture, tools, vacations, and technology are good and enrich our lives. But there comes a point of diminishing returns, when more stuff does not bring more happiness. Imelda Marcos (former first lady of the Philippines) was said to have 2,700 pairs of shoes. It would be stressful for me just trying to decide which pair to wear with such an abundance of choice. Our stuff can suffocate us.

And the stuff that fills life is not just material goods such as shoes, clothes, and electronic gadgets. There are the intangible "things" such as time, opinions, privacy, social media, and feelings that can muck up our freedom if we cling to them. Overscheduling and overcommitting can strain true happiness. Being consumed with "being right," winning arguments, and getting our way is a path to losing friends and self-respect. Total privacy can be peaceful for a while but lonely over the long haul. Hanging on to feelings of anger or disappointment can poison our human relationships and lead to depression. Who wants that!

I believe that we humans are searching for a life with meaning that truly satisfies. Ultimately it is a spiritual journey even for people not connected to any organized religion. Major world religions consistently reinforce this concept of living lightly and not setting our hearts on accumulating the things of this world. My own Catholic faith continues to steer me in this direction of letting go—when my mind is uncluttered enough to listen.

Uncluttering our lives, both materially and inwardly, can bring us a fuller, more meaningful life and free us to attend to the needs of others. For me, uncluttering began as a Lenten practice of giving things away and evolved into a deeper spiritual journey toward God. But even if you approach the practice merely for pragmatic reasons (being able to find things, getting better organized, and becoming more efficient), it's worth the bother.

We can look at living lightly from several different angles. Here are some that motivated me.

It cleans out my home. For many people this is the starting place, and it may end up being enough. Pruning clutter and unnecessary items from your home is good in itself. It makes it easier to find the things that really matter. It offers a more pleasant environment in which to live. It's easier to dust—for those of us who still dust!

It shares the wealth. If I have enough stuff that some of it is unnecessary, a duplication, or is simply being saved for a rainy day, I am wealthy. I may not *feel* wealthy—compared to Warren Buffet or even my neighbor—but I have extra stuff. It is both satisfying and a moral imperative to share what I don't need with those who need it. My extra jacket, set of sheets, or tools can be used by someone who needs it now. It is only fair and just to share with others what I no longer need.

It's good for the Earth. By recycling not only our garbage but also our usable goods and giving them to others, we lighten the load on the environment. We reduce the energy needed to produce new goods and transport them. We create less waste. Living more lightly on our earth is environmentally sound. It benefits all of us by contributing to a greener, leaner planet that's healthier for all life.

It's spiritually fulfilling. I started my effort to downsize my life as a practical way to enter into the religious season of Lent. I thought that giving away many of my possessions would be a worthy way to experience this sacrificial season. What I found in the process was that I not only cleaned out my home and did some good for others, but letting go of stuff also changed my attitude toward my possessions and helped me clarify my true priorities.

It is a spiritual challenge to put our stuff and our lives at the service of others. As a Christian I see this way of life as a gospel imperative, but it's not easily accomplished. Other religions move believers in the same direction. Uncluttering for the purpose of seeing life's deeper meaning transcends any particular faith. People of good will generally yearn for a reason to get up in the morning beyond accumulating more stuff. We want to make a positive difference in our world. Learning to live more generously, humbly, and lightly is a way to do this.

How Much Is Enough? How Much Is Too Much?

It's dangerous to pose these questions. A young family I know decided to move into a Catholic Worker house to minister to the homeless families that stayed there. It was a risk. Were they being responsible parents to their own children? We own a whirlpool tub. Is this an unnecessary extravagance or justifiable hydrotherapy? The answers are personal and it's easy to be judgmental of others or too hard on ourselves. We must always be cautious about judging another person's luxury. True, Marcos's 2,700 pairs of shoes seems extravagant by anyone's standards, but how many shoes are enough? Where does a conscientious person draw the line?

Since it's always risky to compare our possessions with others', I don't postulate income levels or specific things to buy or not buy. I offer ten Rules of Thumb that my family and various friends have developed over decades of trying to answer these questions.

Rules of Thumb for Living Lightly

1. Living in destitution is not a virtue; helping people out of destitution is.
2. Be prudent, responsible, and wise.
3. Be generous, unencumbered, and fair.
4. The less I have, the less I have to guard, clean, and repair.
5. If I don't need it now (or soon), can I give it to someone who does?
6. Spend in order to save.
7. Decide which technologies save time, energy, and money—and which ones waste time, energy, and money.
8. Let go of anger, grudges, and compulsions to lighten the heart.
9. Smile and laugh more.
10. Forgive others. Forgive myself. It lifts the spirit.

By the end of this book and your own journey of striving to live more lightly, you will probably have less stuff and more questions. This is good. The questions lead us to a deeper understanding of our lives' purposes and priorities. It may seem morbid, but I find it very freeing to ponder the Scripture, "[Remember Susan,] you are dust and to dust you will return" (Genesis 3:19). I have no proof that there is an afterlife, but it is something I have chosen to believe. Either way, the things of this world will be of no use to me after death. The only thing that will truly count is how I have loved and cared for others.

2

How Much Is Enough?

If you have food in the refrigerator, clothes on your back, a roof overhead and a place to sleep, . . . you are more comfortable than 75% of the people in this world.

If you have money in the bank, in your wallet, and spare change in a dish someplace, . . . you are among the top 8% of the world's wealthy.

If you can read this, you are more blessed than over two billion people in the world who cannot read at all.

—from The State of the Village Report (2011), original version by Donella H. Meadows

The conventional answer to the question "How much is enough?" is that a person never has enough. Perhaps it goes back to prehistoric times when our ancestors couldn't be assured that they would find enough food to eat each day. Although some people on earth still live with constant uncertainty about their next meal, this is not the case for many of us who live in developed countries. If you can afford to buy and read this book, chances are you have the necessities to sustain life.

But just staying alive does not automatically translate into leading a fulfilling, meaningful life. It seems fair to say that the following would qualify as the basics for a decent human life in a developed country:

- Enough food to stay healthy and the means to cook it
- Enough clothing to stay warm and that is appropriate for my work

- Housing that is safe and clean with enough space for some privacy
- Enough education for the kind of work I want to do and the tools with which to do it.
- Access to affordable health care
- Some discretionary money for treats or recreation
- A job to pay for the above necessities

Of course there's great latitude in the kind of food we eat, the style of clothes we wear, and the quality of housing we live in. In fact, a frighteningly high percentage of people who live in poverty also struggle with obesity, which is related not to the amount of food they eat but the poor quality of affordable food available to them. Clothing is not just a matter of staying warm but of personal expression as well. A home is not just a place in which to escape the elements but also a dwelling that we hope is in a safe environment.

During the active parenting stage of our life, Jim and I of necessity accumulated a lot of stuff. Kids need clothes (which they constantly outgrow), food (which is consumed quickly), and shelter (they might like to subsist on sleepovers, but eventually the other parents would wonder). Like any kids, ours asked for, and often whined for, a lot more: brand name shoes, equipment and lessons for their interests, cell phones and whatever the latest technology offered. Add to that their finicky eating habits, and where do you draw the line? Is it okay to take the family out to an expensive restaurant, or must we always be deferring to mac-and-cheese and other such cheaper fare? Are two pairs of shoes (one for work and one for play) enough? Most of us have much more than these basics, but living lightly does not mean living in destitution. Hence, **Rule of Thumb #1: Living in destitution is not a virtue; helping people out of destitution is**.

People who live in slums and wear raggedy clothing because they have no choice genuinely do not have enough. I grew up in an affluent family and had compassion for those in need but little direct experience of poverty. Following my idealistic college days, my husband, Jim, and I decided to live in a poor inner-city neighborhood in order to unite our lives with the hardships of others and to better understand their needs.

We experienced diminished city services such as police response time, neighborhood litter, and substandard housing. I learned the neighborhood gossip at the corner Laundromat. I learned not to sit in my car reading a map while teenagers walked by because it was a dead giveaway that our home would be vacant for several hours. A burglary followed. The police said the best protection was to get a big dog. We did, but the burglars got smarter and fed the dog meat from the refrigerator when they returned for the next break-in. We became siren deaf because we heard emergency vehicles so often. We only noticed them when visitors would comment on it.

We were young and idealistic, so we accepted the hardships as the price of compassion. Besides, we were buffered by the realization that we had our education and could move out whenever we chose. We plunged into working with the neighborhood community council to get to know our neighbors better, and we joined with them in lobbying the city for better services. Walking our baby provided a natural conversation opener with people on the street. It was an exciting and meaningful time for us because we felt we were contributing to the betterment of our community. But as our first child grew older, I started paying attention to the local schools and wondered what we would do when he was ready for kindergarten.

That decision was finessed when we decided to move to another state to explore new job possibilities. Our new neighborhood had less crime and housing blight because it was a federally subsidized housing cooperative, but I continued to be aware through language, education, and parenting practices that I had many more resources to help me face the challenges of life in a low-income area than many of our neighbors had. When a new job led to another move and our family and income grew, health and safety became higher priorities for us. Did we cop out by moving into a more stable neighborhood and up the socioeconomic ladder?

I don't think so. The causes of poverty are complex and there are many ways to respond to the needs of those who are struggling. Some of us have the responsibility to educate and empower people to get jobs that pay a living wage. Others work through politics to make just laws that provide a level playing field. Others work for nonprofits that help people better themselves. Some people are called to analyze why poverty continues. Still others donate money or volunteer time. These responses are all good and necessary, but it doesn't help the conscientious person know what his or her unique "enough" is.

Having the responsibility for raising healthy children taught me that "enough" doesn't require that we live barely above the poverty line. It's not bad or selfish to have a decent home, a car, furniture, tools, computers, and cell phones, or to go on vacations. If we have come by our incomes honestly, and if we are not slaves to conspicuous consumption, then we need not flog ourselves for having good fortune. So, problem of how much is enough solved? Not quite. We need **Rule of Thumb #2: Be prudent, responsible, and wise**.

Being Prudent

I could save money by not having health or life insurance. Maybe I'd be lucky and not get a serious illness or have an accident. If I do get sick, however, it puts the burden on others to pay for my care. That's not fair. I may decide that getting a simple vaccine to prevent a disease is like playing God and I will trust God to take care of me. My view is that God gives us the intelligence and resources to learn how to prevent many diseases. To ignore those talents disrespects God's gifts to us.

Prudence says that when possible I should buy clothes and other goods that will last. It may cost a little more in the short run, but it's good stewardship. Likewise, having some savings for an emergency is not frivolous but good planning. Prudence is taking an umbrella when rain is forecast.

Prudence means appreciating that most of the things of this world are good and enjoyable. Use them in moderation. There is no need to disdain comfort, useful or beautiful possessions, and uplifting recreation as long as these purchases are in harmony with two basic values: *People are more important than things* and *Time is more important than money*. We'll talk more about these values in chapter 8, which deals with the intangible stuff of our lives.

Being Responsible

As a parent, I'm responsible for the safety and education of my children. For most people this means we don't relocate to an environment known to be unsafe, whether that's a poverty-stricken neighborhood or another country for the purpose of missionary work. Such radical moves aren't necessarily wrong but need to be taken with great care and prayer. For most people, living in a safe neighborhood, having a decent job, and providing common everyday comforts is how we take responsibility for our family.

There is also something I call "creature comfort creep." I was satisfied with my first cell phone that simply made calls until I started seeing people take photos with their phones. Later I was impressed with how our kids would look up information on their smart phones when I still needed to find an Internet connection for my laptop. Whatever lifestyle I currently have seems fine until I start to see people around me having more, or see ads for things I don't have. I may buy just a few more things—and these things then define the new normal. The ante keeps rising.

One way I've discovered to guard against this virtual blindness is to keep grounded by making contact with a variety of people, particularly those who have less than I have, no matter what that income level is. I might do this by participating in programs that address hunger or homelessness. One simple way to meet a cross-section of people—at least in larger cities—is to use public transportation. Sharing and honoring the experiences of human diversity can teach me about life beyond my personal sphere, and it can make my assessments of "enough" more honest.

However, when I see up close how difficult some people's lives are, I am tempted to feel guilty that I have a decent home, a good education, and a job that's a good fit for my skills and gifts. It won't help anyone's situation for me to deny my own good fortune, be dismissive about it, or punish myself for my situation. What I can do is allow my developing awareness of others' needs to be a trigger for me—a prompt that will move me to advocate against the injustices that I see. The trigger may be a call to live more simply. Or, when being brutally honest with myself, sometimes I have come to realize that it would be irresponsible to substantially change my lifestyle. It has been essential for me to grow in self-awareness and to consult with other people connected to me, such as children who depended on me.

A friend of mine felt very strongly about two issues: malnourished inner-city populations and the system by which most beef, chicken, pork, and other animal products come to the average grocery aisle. She was determined to stop eating "factory meat" produced in conditions cruel to the animals, brutal to the environment, and in many cases dangerously unhealthy to consumers. The problem was, when she bought meat from a farmer's market in her area, she sometimes had to pay three times what she would have at supermarkets. She knew that many of the people who bought the bargain meat could never pay farmers' market prices. Should she dine on what others could not afford—even though by doing so she was supporting a system that she felt, was ethically much better for everyone? Here's the conclusion she came to:

> Years ago, organic fruits and vegetables were hard to come by, and they were expensive. But a core group of people who could afford to support the organic market did so, and as a result, you can now buy truly organic produce even in the low-end discount stores. Organic has become popular, and the big corporate stores pay attention to that, so they are gradually making more ethical decisions about fruits and vegetables. If I can afford to pay double or triple for pork chops or ground beef, then in a way, I feel a responsibility to continue supporting better farming practices. In time, I believe that these kinder, more environmentally responsible methods of raising animals and providing meat to consumers will gain momentum.

Being Wise

As **Rule of Thumb #6 states, Spend in order to save.** It may seem like a luxury, but in reality, it's being wise. We insulated our house to save on future energy bills. We sometimes paid more to buy durable toys. (This lesson came from buying a cheap plastic kid's swimming pool one summer that barely lasted the summer.) Others may look at your purchases and judge that you are extravagant. You may wonder yourself if you should give the money to charitable causes instead. These are thorny personal decisions. So, pray, summon up your wisdom, and consult with other wise and thoughtful people; then make the decision you can live with. As for what others think of you, maybe they missed the part of Rule of Thumb #10 about forgiving others and not judging.

This Rule of Thumb #2 about being prudent, responsible, and wise lays the foundation for deciding what is enough; however, guidelines by nature are general and open to a lot of interpretation and even self-deception. Stay spiritually centered so as not to judge others, feel deprived, or lose heart for the journey.

First Steps and Big Steps

Light and easy

Make a list of what material things you consider are absolutely essential for your life and happiness. Would people close to you have similar lists? How would your list differ from someone living in poverty or in great wealth? Do you know people in either of these extremes?

Extreme lightness

Beyond the absolute necessities of life, what would be the most difficult discretionary possession for you to give away? What's keeping you from letting it go?

For Meditation

Keep your lives free from the love of money, and be content with what you have; for he has said, "I will never leave you or forsake you."

—Hebrews 13:5

For Reflection or Discussion

- What is my most prized material possession? What can't I live without?
- Do I consider myself a prudent and responsible person or more of a happy-go-lucky free spirit? What are the pros and cons of each?
- Have I ever had to scrimp to make ends meet? Go into debt for rent or medicine?
- How would I know when I have enough income?
- What would be the basic possessions I need for a decent life?

3

How Much Is Too Much?

Ted always buys the latest laptop computer, smart phone, and has lots of photographic equipment. It's expensive but he makes a good income and playing with technology is his hobby. Is it too much? Should he wait for sales?

If you thought the "How much is enough?" question was hard, the "How much is too much?" question is even more challenging. The common answer is that *too much* is always a little more than what I have. In most minds, *too much* usually hangs out there with people who are outlandishly wealthy and conspicuous consumers, far from ordinary people like me.

On a whim I did the Global Rich List calculator for my household (www.globalrichlist.com). I don't think of myself as rich and I didn't come out in the top 1 percent of rich people; but I was closer than I expected. It was sobering. Since this is a worldwide comparison, it doesn't consider the lower cost of living in developing countries. Still it made me stop and ponder. "How much is too much?"

Once we've let go of the fantasy that there is never *too much*, we can start to look honestly at our own lifestyle and possessions. Perhaps indeed you are just scraping by, or you're unemployed and desperately looking for work. In this case it is only right that those who have more should apply the last chapter's Rule of Thumb #1, about helping people out of destitution, and give you a leg up. For the rest of us, it's a matter of cultivating the virtues that help us guard against thinking that *too much* is always a little more than what I have.

It may sound counterintuitive, but many people are discovering that having less is not a hardship but a blessing. The words of minimalist blogger, Joshua Becker, echo mine: "Since choosing to live with less, we have experienced numerous unexpected benefits. We have more time, more energy, more freedom, and more money to pursue what is most important to us. Owning less means less cleaning, less burden, less anxiety, and less stress" (www.becomingminimalist.com). Here's where we learn the wisdom of **Rule of Thumb #3: Be generous, unencumbered, and fair**.

At first blush, giving stuff away may seem like a burden or sacrifice. My experience, however, has been that it has been freeing and satisfying.

Being Generous

It is incumbent upon those of us who have money or goods beyond the squishy, *just enough* bar, to be generous. This is what prompted my original decision to give away one thing a day for forty days of Lent and then extend it for 365 days. This resulted in my giving away more than 1,200 items the first year. Some were very small, like pencils and vegetables, but others were more major, like luggage and silver. I realize that not everyone has so much stuff that they could give away one thing a day; but it fit my stage of life and circumstances. And there was an unintended side effect. Deciding what to let go of and what to keep forced me to assess daily why I wanted to keep certain items. Which things did I really need? Which did I want for nostalgic reasons? Which were just hanging around, stored, or completely forgotten? I decided that it was okay to keep some things that others might consider luxuries (electric toothbrush, L. L. Bean jacket). After defining the basics for myself (plus a few luxuries), I developed some criteria for what to keep versus how much to give away to others.

With money:

- I've found that the biblical ten percent tithe of income to charity is a way to assuage the uncertainty I often feel about whether I am donating enough. Of course, ten percent of a meager income is a greater sacrifice than a millionaire's ten percent.
- Spend in order to save. Buying quality and energy-efficient appliances and cars, and doing home repairs will save money and the environment over the long haul.

With possessions:

- If I have extras or unnecessary items that I can share or give away to others, what's stopping me? If I already do this, am I doing it with pride or with humility?

With time:

- Time is money. Sometimes it's worth "wasting" it on others. Spend time with an elderly neighbor who is unable to get out and socialize much; give time to a local tutoring program or volunteer in some way at a neighborhood school that is short on supplies and helpers; assist people for whom English is a second language in filling out forms, developing resumes, or otherwise navigating paperwork or a system.
- On the other hand, I've learned that I don't have to bake cookies for every school or charitable event. Baking is a burden for me. Someone else can do it. My time is better spent buying the treat and bringing a less frazzled presence to a social gathering.

Being generous sounds so obvious and honorable it's hard to argue with. But then there's the question of finding the best means of getting your excess to someone who needs it. We're inundated with pleas from charitable organizations—which ones are the best at helping people? Or, who are the people close by who could use your assistance?

If your normal routine does not bring you into contact with people you consider "needy," either your movements are too limited or your definition of neediness is. In whatever environment you find yourself, assume that some person in the room is in need. Few people today are free of financial worry and insecurity. Someone at your office is drowning in medical bills; someone else is overwhelmed by a legal situation such as divorce, custody disputes, or elder care. If you are at all involved in social justice ministries in your church or community, you will find opportunities to make meaningful contact with people who struggle because they live in poverty, or are trying to get free of addiction, or are trying to make up for lost time with their education.

Look at your own interests, and then find a cause or ministry in which your particular gifts fit. Are you a gardener? Where's the nearest community garden project? Do you like to feed people? Find the local soup kitchen or neighborhood pantry. Are you a people person? Look for programs in which you can help advocate for those fighting unjust landlords or who need help maintaining contact with their families while being incarcerated.

One evening we got an 11:00 p.m. phone call from a homeless family. It was a surprise but it wasn't a random call for help. It came after time spent helping a friend with her foster daughter, which evolved into transporting the pregnant mother for medical care after she left home. This then developed into helping the husband get a part-time job. Eventually, it meant sharing our home. Things happen when you let yourself form authentic relationships—when you become friends.

Being Unencumbered

Having too much stuff clutters a home, making it unattractive and difficult to find things. We may feel compelled to protect it with keys and alarms that require remembering long strings of numbers or passwords. Cleaning around stuff can be a hassle. Silver needs polishing. (Although our daughter swears that if she ever gets any silver, she will consider polishing it a relaxing therapy.) Sorting and storing stuff can be an art form for the creative and provide jobs for professional organizers, but it still complicates life.

Having too much stuff also requires a lot of our mental, emotional, and physical time. We have to organize it, care for it, think about it, rearrange it, worry about it, and then reorganize it again. Think of how involved you can become simply repainting one room of your house or buying one new piece of furniture. Suddenly you're evaluating everything else about the room. Maybe you need a few more shelves over there, or a nicer area rug over here, and how about getting a better coffee table to go with the new couch? And once this room looks better, what about the other rooms? This can become circular and never ending, and the more possessions we have, the more loops can develop.

Beyond a plethora of physical possessions, too much stuff can also clutter our minds. "Where did I store those outgrown toddler clothes, the kids' art projects from last year, and those Halloween decorations?" "Which of my ten scarves will best accent my mauve suit?" (If you don't know what mauve is, you're probably unfettered by the fashion police and can dress in unbridled freedom.)

Being Fair

As the Occupy movement has reminded us, it's just not fair that a small percentage of the people hold the vast majority of wealth and decision-making power. To their credit, a number of the super-rich recognize this and have stood in solidarity with the ninety-nine percent. But those of us who are not super-rich still need to think about what's fair. We may have worked hard to get the jobs and income we enjoy, but some of our privilege is also due to being born into the right family, race, country, and era, and having parents who valued education and had the resources to help us get a good start. We may be blessed with strong bodies, able minds, and healthy genes. Not everyone starts out with all these advantages.

It is only fair that to those who have been given much, much is to be expected (see Luke 12:48). So, how is a person who has a reasonable income called to be fair? The following insights and practices have been growing in me:

- Pay taxes with gratitude that I have an income to tax. As Justice Oliver Wendell Holmes said, "Taxes are the price we pay for a civilized society."
- Look upon opportunities to fund worthy causes not as *charity* but as *justice*; a way of giving back.
- Evaluate the impact that the things I own and my lifestyle have on planet earth. Am I using more than my fair share of energy resources? Is my transportation environmentally friendly?
- Stay in solidarity with people who are marginalized by staying informed, praying, fasting, and participating in social justice endeavors.

And then there's tough love. Those with a compassionate heart often feel pulled to empty our pockets when we see pictures of starving children, people with terrible diseases, or abject poverty. This is good, but not good enough. The responsible giver must make the effort to discern the best way to help and that's not always to throw money at a situation. The money is essential, but our dollars should be used judiciously to help people get out of destitution. This means not just bailing somebody out but helping them work toward long-term change. This might translate into helping an individual learn to budget and prioritize. But it might also mean putting pressure on power structures to change so that oppressive systems are dismantled. A budget is irrelevant if, at the end of a sixty-hour work week, the paycheck and benefits fall below what is necessary for basic living.

One personal experience with learning the non-monetary cost of helping started with that 11:00 p.m. call from the young unemployed couple we had been helping with baby clothes and transportation. They said they had to leave their home immediately. They were living with newly made acquaintances in temporary housing. The wife said that their new "friends" were doing drugs, and they feared for their safety. What if the police raided the place and their baby was taken away from them? Jim and I looked at each other and decided we needed time to think before inviting them to come live with us. That was prudence kicking in. We said we'd call them the next morning.

Having been a social worker for many years, I knew how easily temporary shelter could become long term, and we had settled into a comfortable lifestyle with just the two of us. This would mean reviving our child-care days since the baby was only six months old. We knew of an agency that housed homeless families, but it would take a while to check it out and make arrangements. We said they could stay with us for two weeks while we worked out the details for more permanent housing. We ended up extending their stay much longer, but one of the things I learned is that helping was more complicated than I had anticipated. We spent hours taking them to social services, working out immigration technicalities and employment searches. Different parenting styles wore on us as we wondered how much to interfere when the baby was crying and what kind of house rules to impose on "guests."

This is hard work and might not feel like living lightly, because having resources to help can be a burden. It's not easy to help in the best way. It takes creativity, shrewdness, and walking as a friend beside those in need, sometimes for a long time. It is the responsibility of having more than enough. In the end, however, tough love can be kindness, since it creates lasting change.

Still not sure of what's fair? Kindness is the bottom line.

Consider **Rule of Thumb #4: The less I have, the less I have to guard, clean, and repair**. Stuff can take time. It's not just the time it takes to care for and repair our stuff, but also the time it takes to earn the money to buy it.

It reminds me of our daughter's Peace Corps experience. I visited her in her small African village, and at first blush this Malian community appeared primitive to my eyes. I wondered how the people survived. They didn't have electricity or running water, yet every day they stopped for tea and a nap in the heat of the afternoon. Most spoke more than one language, and they had time to visit and dance in the evenings. I watched a woman do her daily chore of pounding millet to make flour. I conjectured about how modern machinery could do it more efficiently and enable her to be more productive. Perhaps she could even start a business making flour for the whole village and increase her income by selling it to nearby villages. Eventually she would have enough money to retire to a life of ease—in which she could drink tea and nap in the afternoon and dance at night.

Or consider the parent who diligently works overtime to provide the "extras" for the family—a nicer car, a plush vacation, an entertainment center with lots of media—except the father is never around to attend his kid's games or the mother can't take time for a hike in the woods. Our own kids used to complain that we didn't make enough money for their tastes and that we should stop this silly job-sharing arrangement. Now that they are young adults, their opinions have changed. Now they say that our presence was more valuable than more presents would have been.

Long hours at work can steal time from our families, and for what? To get more stuff? Freeing up time can mean either working longer to pay for hired help to do menial chores or it can mean working shorter and doing those chores yourself—even better, with your family.

First Steps and Big Steps

Light and easy

Identify at least one possession that is really more than you need. Maybe it's a duplicate, or too big or too small. Let it go.

Educate your mind and heart about the needs of people living at or below the poverty level. Read a book (*When Helping Hurts*, Corbett/Fikkert, *Poverty of Spirit*, Metz, *The Jesuit Guide to (Almost) Everything: A Spirituality for Real Life*, Martin), go to a movie (*The Grapes of Wrath*, *The Line*), or attend a civic meeting dealing with housing or social services.

Extreme lightness

You probably know many people who have a lot more money and possessions than you do. You might even feel rather superior in how you've reduced your possessions already. Let go of comparing yourself to others. Give yourself the freedom to enter into the rest of this book with an open heart to what you should hang on to and what you should let go of.

For Meditation

Be on your guard against all kinds of greed; for one's life does not consist in the abundance of possessions. Then he told them a parable: "The land of a rich man produced abundantly. And he thought to himself, 'What should I do, for I have no place to store my crops?' Then he said, 'I will do this: I will pull down my barns and build larger ones, and there I will store all my grain and my goods. And I will say to my soul, Soul, you have ample goods laid up for many years; relax, eat, drink, be merry.' But God said to him, 'You fool! This very night your life is being demanded of you. And the things you have prepared, whose will they be?'"

—Luke 12:15–20

For Reflection or Discussion

- Is it possible to have too much stuff? How would I recognize that point in myself or others? You know you are too wealthy when . . .

- Think of a time when I had a conflict within myself as to whether to be prudent or generous. Which did I choose and why?

- If I could design a perfect society, how would I balance the needs of the "haves" with the "have nots?" What political solutions seem fair and workable?

4

Consume Less—Save More Money

I'm a pretty frugal, thrifty person by nature. (Our kids have a less flattering word for it: tightwad.) So how did a person who disdained conspicuous consumption since college accumulate all this stuff?

My possessions crept up on me slowly. Many of my goods are indeed good and necessary. But now that I'm downsizing, I'm evaluating more carefully what I do buy, and I'm trying to understand why I've held on to so much. Our culture, however, seduces us to believe that we need "more than enough" to be really happy and to lead a fulfilling life. Fighting the many subliminal messages out there to accumulate more requires a countercultural attitude, self-reflection, and wise mentors.

If you move often or are in the practice of having garage sales, you may not have that many possessions to prune. That's fine. You may, however, want to evaluate what you choose to buy and how much it is based on the most recent style rather than your true preferences and needs.

Connecting to Your Stage of Life

For those in the first half of life

Living on a tight budget during my postcollege and early parenting years forced me to be frugal. Some practices, like using cloth diapers, saved us a lot of money, was ecologically sound, and really no more trouble than doing an extra load of wash each week. Of course, these savings only pertain to the early parenting years. Other practices, such as limiting how often we went out for dinner have become a lifelong habit. The beauty of the first half of life is that it's always easier and more gratifying to splurge occasionally than to become accustomed to a lifestyle of self-indulgence. Consuming less is easier when your friends are also in the early, necessarily frugal phase of life.

For those in the second half of life

By the time we are in the second half of life, we hope to be established in a place that has become a home, one that might be paid off or close to it. With a home we have probably collected many of the possessions we felt we needed. So now, with the exception of having to replace a major appliance, we have acquired much of what we need to live the life we've chosen. The challenge is to moderate spending habits even if we now have discretionary money. Just because I can afford something doesn't mean I must own it. Just because the shoes are appealing doesn't mean I need another pair. Of course an occasional treat is good for the soul. But a treat isn't a treat if you have it every day.

Buy Less

One thing I learned from giving stuff away for a year is that it tamed my appetite for buying stuff. This end can also be achieved by not having any discretionary money to begin with.

Early in our married life, my husband and I recorded every penny we spent, even our parking meter change. This was probably extreme, but it taught us how quickly money can slip through our fingers, and when we totaled up expenditures at the end of each month, we had a sense of those semi-invisible costs such as a snack here and a gadget there. It didn't mean that we stopped making purchases, but it did show us where the black holes were.

Giving stuff away accomplished some of this same purpose. When I would see something in a store and consider buying it, it became automatic for me to ask, "Is this something that I'll just be giving away soon when the charm has worn off?"

But, you say, "Besides food, clothing, and shelter, I need kitchen supplies, tools to repair things, furniture to sit on, and electronics to communicate with the outside world." Of course. This is where the "Spend in order to save" maxim applies. I've learned the hard way that too often my tightwad-self tried to save money by buying something cheap only to end up paying more when I had to replace it prematurely.

Many decorative items fall into this category: temporary decorative disposables. How many Christmas knick-knacks or Halloween decorations are worth the glitz? When we had small children at home, such items played a part in family rituals and were justifiable. Keeping some arts and craft supplies for visiting kids is an important job of grandparents. Being a slave to fads and fashion, however, is a waste—unless it's chocolate.

A variation on the "Buy Less" category is "Buy Used." Thrifty people have been doing this for years through craigslist, eBay, St. Vincent de Paul, and Goodwill. I'm a cautious fan of buying used. If you know your seller and do your research, it's a help. We recently bought a refurbished sewing machine and vacuum cleaner from a local merchant who guarantees his products. We always buy used cars—after our mechanic has checked them out. The temptation is that sometimes a used item seems like such a good deal that we buy too many or we pick up things we don't really need.

When I'm considering buying something new or used, my criteria are:

- Is it necessary?
- Is it of sufficient quality for its purpose?

- Will it last?

Sometimes an item doesn't pass these tests but qualifies for purchase under the Vogt House Rules:

- Will it bring fun into my life in proportion to its cost?
- Will it bring joy to someone else?
- Do I really love it?
- Is it worth the money?

Share, Borrow, and Trade

When trying to buy less, it's helpful to have friends. Friends are wonderful for their own sake, but one happy side effect of friendships, especially long-term ones, is that they provide a community in which to share goods. In such a community you can share, borrow, and trade.

Probably the biggest way this played out for our family was when we downsized to one car. With the kids sprung and both my husband and I working at home, it wasn't that much of a stretch. But there are some times when both of us need to go in different directions at the same time. Although the truly virtuous would take public transportation, it's not always convenient. Our backup is our friends. Their values are similar to ours, and a couple of them live nearby, making it relatively easy to borrow a car. We return the favor by sometimes doing childcare for them, but no one is keeping track—because we're friends.

At other times we've borrowed wheelbarrows and other tools. One of our more creative ventures is that we trade newspapers with a neighbor. They get the local paper and we get a national one. Each day when we've finished reading our respective newspapers, we run across the street and deliver the paper. Saves paper and spreads knowledge. Maybe we even chat. Often my contra-dancing friends and I will trade dresses. It feels like a new dance wardrobe and everybody wins.

I've often thought that not everyone on a street needs their private lawn mower but that might be a little more complicated. Sharing and borrowing require a degree of trust and responsibility, but isn't that implied in the definition of friend? We help each other out.

Eat Less

In its most literal sense, consuming less includes eating less. This certainly applies to junk food, especially in a society such as ours in which obesity has become so prevalent. It often costs more, however, to eat nutritionally, organically, and local. So how do we save money when eating? Mostly, it's by eating in, not out. It's not the quantity of food we eat but the quality that counts. Eating less junk and more nutritious food is also consistent with the spend-in-order-to-save Rule of Thumb #6. Spending the time to cook at home and spending the money to buy less processed or convenience foods can save in the long run. Eating nutritious foods may cost more up front, but these eating habits are bound to prevent expensive health care later.

So how little can we spend on food and still eat nutritiously? I was wondering that when I came across the Food Stamp Challenge. Hmmm, my year of giving away at least one thing a day was over, and I was looking for a new Lenten practice. I reflected that Jesus did a lot of feeding hungry people and curing their illnesses. Perhaps trying to eat on the average Food Stamp budget of $4.50/day would be an act of solidarity with those who don't have a choice but to buy the cheapest food. It would probably also teach me some things about myself. It seemed like an appropriate Lenten effort.

How did it work out? It wasn't easy, but with a great deal of attention to simple meals, sales, and careful planning, we got by. I wouldn't want to do if for more than six weeks. Jim and I compromised some of our principles about buying organic. We ate no desserts or snacks, little meat, drank only water (except for morning OJ) and ate a lot of macaroni and cheese. Most of our budget went for fruits and vegetables because we weren't willing to jeopardize our health for the sake of an artificial experiment. Although neither Jim nor I drink much alcohol, we do periodically enjoy a glass of wine. Of course, we couldn't afford it on our Food Stamp budget, but sometimes we would be visiting someone who would offer us some wine. We rationalized that a little spirits (wine/beer) can lighten one's spirit. Jesus drank wine with his friends. We should do no less. The tricky question is, How much is "a little?"

I didn't lose or gain weight, but I did gain some human and spiritual insights. I became much more personally connected with the Corporal Work of Mercy, "I was hungry and you gave me food" (Matthew 25:35). I started identifying with people all over the world who experience *real* hunger. Mostly I gained understanding and compassion for those for whom a Food Stamp budget is an ongoing reality rather than a six-week experiment—people who don't have the luxury of choice. They have to constantly juggle whether to buy the cheaper food or the healthier food. They don't have the luxury of driving around town to farmer's markets or sales. They might not have the time or education to do the painstaking research we did to calculate the best deal and cheap but nutritious recipes. They may not have a spouse who likes to cook.

Is a Food Stamp Challenge in your future? Read more about it on my blog. Try it. You might like it.

Consume Less Packaging

I'm amazed at how even a dedicated recycler inevitably consumes a lot of nonconsumable packaging. I already take cloth bags to stores and repeat the mantra, "I don't need a bag" to sales clerks. A few times this has resulted in my carrying four or five loose items out of the store because I left my bag in the car, but generally I feel honorable about this and suck it up. The hardest part has been those stubborn items (often electronics) that come overpackaged, often in hard to cut plastic clam shells. Chapter 9 will delve more deeply into wasting fewer resources including packaging, but since you're reading this now, at least keep watch over what packaging accompanies your purchases. Awareness is the first step.

Decisions about what to buy and what not to buy are complex and often emotional. Although I accumulated a lot of stuff over the years, I might have collected much more had it not been for attitudes I developed during my countercultural college years. Here my natural frugality met my old 1960s values of simple lifestyle and not going along with the crowd. Granted, there's some level of conformity in an entire group that decides to be countercultural! Not being a slave to fashion came pretty easily to me; it helped that as a social worker and later a church employee, I didn't have a lot of money to spend. And I didn't generally hang around with people who were hypersensitive to fashion or trends.

It went deeper, however, than necessity and personal style. As I was exposed to people who truly were poor and I saw their hardships, it touched my heart. This was reinforced by my continuing spiritual journey in which I read so many Scriptures about the need not to cling to the material things of this world—the Gospel accounts of the lilies of the field, the rich young man, the widow's mite, and the rich landowner who hoarded his wealth. The biblical imperative of cultivating a preferential option for the poor gnawed at me. I didn't expect to "leave *everything*," but I didn't want to go away sad as the rich young man did (Mark 10:22). I started to recognize fads as temporary and "keeping up with the Joneses" as an unnecessary goal. Neither was worth my hard-earned money or my soul. Developing an attitude of detachment and generosity balanced my wants and penny-pinching.

First Steps and Big Steps

Light and easy

Other than food and transportation, try buying nothing for a
week. Or, if that seems too daunting, try this for a day or two.
Go ahead and pay bills, but buy nothing new, even with a
credit card. You may have to cheat if an unexpected required
expense comes up, such as a doctor's visit or emergency car
repair. The point is not to deprive yourself completely but to
delay gratification long enough to discern whether a particular
want is really necessary; the goal is to open your mind to mod-
erating your lifestyle. You might also choose to read an article
or book about people who have simplified their lives. (See bibliography for ideas.)

Extreme lightness

Other than food, transportation, and existing financial com-
mitments such as rent/mortgage, Internet/phone bills, insurance, and so forth, try buying nothing for a six-week period;
you might do this during Lent. Another option would be to
take the Food Stamp Challenge described on my blog
(www.SusanVogt.net/blog). If you're in the market for a car,
house, or major appliance, evaluate the necessity of the purchase and if it meets the "Spend in order to save" criteria. Can
you purchase a smaller or more energy-efficient item? What's
your biggest money hog that's not a necessity? What fad or
gadget do you continue to buy but could live without? (Do alco-
holic beverages or specialty coffee count? Maybe.)

For Meditation

[Job] said, "Naked I came from my mother's womb, and
naked shall I return there; the Lord gave, and the Lord has
taken away; blessed be the name of the Lord."

—Job 1:21

For Reflection or Discussion

- What are some of my best strategies for saving money?
- When have I experienced spending money in order to save money? How did it work out for me?
- Have I ever had a bad experience with someone who borrowed something from me? If a similar situation came up again, how would I handle it?
- Read the scriptural stories about Job (above), the lilies of the field (Matthew 6:25–34), the rich young man (Mark 10:17–31), the widow's mite (Mark 12:41–44), and the rich landowner (Luke 12:15–21). Which one speaks to me most compellingly? Do I have another favorite Scripture that guides what I consume?

5

Hang on to Less — Become More Generous, Feel Freer

Clara's children are in their early twenties, but she has carefully been saving their baby clothes and toys for the grandchildren she hopes to have one day. Her church just announced that they are sponsoring an unwed mother who needs a lot of these things. Save or let go?

Many of us have a natural inclination to save things for a rainy day. Indeed, there is virtue to this predisposition since there are a fair number of rainy days in life. Often it is the responsible thing to do. Many virtues, however, turn into vices when taken to an extreme—I sometimes call vices "virtues on steroids." When saving or protecting my excess meets the need of my neighbor *right now*, generosity will bring less regret and lighten one's spirit.

Now's the time for **Rule of Thumb #5: If I don't need it now (or soon), can I give it to someone who does?** So, what don't you need? When I looked around my own home with this question in mind, I had three goals:

1. To let go of things I no longer needed that were cluttering my home. (I had just spent way too much time trying, unsuccessfully, to find a jacket that one of our sons swore he left somewhere in the house.) Stuffed closets and clutter are not conducive to locating things easily or keeping a light spirit.

2. To give these things to people who needed them more than I did. At the time, we were housing a homeless couple, and I was aware of how few clothes these young parents had for their baby while I was still saving hand-me-downs for my potential grandchildren.

3. To learn how living more lightly might deepen my spirituality and lead me into a more meaningful, generous way of life. A sobering idea to reflect upon: Jesus saved people, not stuff.

Living lightly certainly involved more than cleaning out my home, but it seemed easiest to start with concrete actions that were visible and measurable—dealing with the stuff in front of me. I started with the bedroom because that's where I was standing and it held most of my clothes. But our house is large, and I had accumulated a lot of stuff. I needed a plan and a motivation. The immediate motivation was Lent. The plan was a forty-day strategy.

A Forty-Day Strategy

Research tells us that it takes repetition to establish a habit and that forty days is a good length of time to help a habit stick. I decided to give away at least one thing each of the forty days of Lent. This made sense to me; Lent is a sacrificial season for Christians, and it was a time commitment that seemed manageable to me. To stay motivated and honest, I wrote regular blog posts about the experience. Another self-improvement principle is that telling another person that you are going on a diet or plan to stop smoking increases your chances of being faithful to your commitment.

Perhaps you don't need the structure of forty days, but human nature being what it is, it's easy to procrastinate until one day, some-day, turns into never. What we choose to let go of, however, depends a lot on our stage of life.

Connecting to Your Stage of Life

For those in the first half of life

Perhaps you haven't accumulated enough yet to require pruning your goods. Or perhaps you are saving things to be reused by younger children. This is good. But do you really need those high school term papers, outdated clothes, a cell phone that doesn't even take a photo, or sports memorabilia from a team from your distant past?

For those in the second half of life

Most of this chapter may be especially appropriate for you. Pass on those baby items. It's all right to keep a few toys and clothes for visiting children and grandchildren. Use the wisdom you've gained about the true value of things to let go of the superfluous.

Clothes

Although there is a wide range of things you might choose to give away, clothes are something that everyone has. But we tend to get attached to our clothes. How much is enough is very subjective. I have a good friend, a distinguished judge, who claimed he only needed two pairs of shoes: one for dress and a pair of athletic shoes for everything else. Maybe an ultrafrugal male can pull this off, but I couldn't. I mean, I don't *want* to. So, I was thinking about shoes when I embarked upon my giveaway project.

Since clothes are generally in the same closet as shoes, clothes became my focus for the first couple of weeks. Clothes are not only for warmth and modesty; they are also a big part of our identity. Our culture emphasizes changing styles and uses sexy clothing to sell products, but putting together an attractive outfit and having comfortable clothes that fit can be a joy and a creative expression of self. So how are folks who want to lighten up their clothes closet to proceed?

I started with the letter "S." I didn't intend to start with any particular letter but I had just read an article on the Soles4Souls Web site about how the average American owns thirteen pairs of shoes. Even though I didn't see myself getting down to two pairs, I figured I was probably under thirteen and could go lower. Wrong! When I added up all my shoes (including slippers and boots), it came to thirty pairs. I was horrified! I pruned it down to thirteen, but I was not happy about being average. In a typical week I wear only four pair. That was the first day of giveaways.

I then graduated to other closet items. That meant shirts, skirts, suits, slacks, sweaters, socks, scarves, and sleepwear. There were other pieces of clothing that didn't start with "S" but I noticed the similarity in hindsight. It took me about eleven days to go through my clothes. I didn't count Sundays since I figured that was a day to rest and took the day off to ponder the meaning of what I was doing.

Shirts: I discovered that it was hard to pick just one category like "shirts" to get rid of. Some shirts or tops go with particular slacks or skirts, and it doesn't make sense to discard one without knowing if I'd keep items that coordinate with it. Clothing is like a family system. Each piece has a relationship with other pieces. No shirt is an island.

Skirts/Dresses: Since I've primarily been working from home for the past seven years, I don't need to dress up very often, and that's fine with me. It saves time and money spent on a professional wardrobe. But I had never pruned my professional clothes from my closet. Skirts and dresses were the beginning. Choosing to get rid of some was not a difficult decision. They were pretty outdated anyway, although the poodle skirt made for a good costume.

Suits: Then it got a little harder. Although my typical daily wardrobe consists of jeans and a turtleneck, I do need to have some professional outfits for speaking engagements. A while ago, the fashion police, aka my daughter, informed me that my wardrobe really needed a makeover if I wanted to have credibility with the younger generation of couples and parents. So I have a few stock outfits that I use for travel and speaking. I also want to keep that black suit that's perfect for funerals. As my mother says, "At my age I'm going to more and more funerals."

Slacks/Pants: How many pairs of khaki slacks does a person need? Well, more than one, I guess, since I could only get myself down to three: one dress pair for summer, one dress pair for winter, and one casual pair. I justify these (plus my two pairs of black slacks) by claiming them as my all-purpose travel/speaking uniform since I can match them with different tops and have a variety of outfits. Sounds reasonable to me.

Sweaters: Now here we have some serious bulk. Not only did I have the sweaters I wore on a daily basis, but I rediscovered a stash of sweaters I had stored under the bed. There was the Kelly green one that I only wore on St. Patrick's Day since green isn't really my color; ditto for the red Christmas sweater. I kept asking myself, *Is it fair to hang on to a sweater that I wear only once a year if someone else is cold now?*

Scarves/Jewelry: One of my packing strategies for trips is to take several scarves so I can make three outfits out of one. Scarves are also a small and light accessory which helps me fit everything into a carry-on—a constant goal of mine. In reviewing my scarves and jewelry, however, I did find some that I no longer wear.

Sleepwear and underwear: I needed to face the issue of the propriety of giving away personal items like underwear, even if it's clean and in good condition. I decided to pitch my sagging panty hose and tights, although a blog reader later asked for them to stuff her craft projects. The questions that this category raised for me were:

- Do any women wear slips anymore?

- Why do I have a bikini that I wouldn't dare wear anymore and a swim cap that nobody but Olympic swimmers wear these days?

One thing I learned in going through all my clothes was that it not only took time to decide what I was willing to part with, I also had to assess

- the cleanliness of items
- whether it was worth mending that broken zipper
- whether I would ever lose that extra ten pounds so I could fit into a perfectly good, but a little snug suit
- how long it would take the fashion cycle to return to bell-bottoms

It takes time to wash clothes in order to be a responsible giver. It takes skill to replace a zipper. (I didn't.) It takes honesty to admit that after four children, ten extra pounds is not bad and I'll probably not lose it. Bell-bottoms will come back as soon as I give them away.

Clothes pruning strategies:

- Many people use the "one in, one out" system to keep control of their closets. Our daughter keeps only a limited number of hangers. When they are full, it's time to purge.
- Another person used hangers by turning them all toward the wall. Each time she wore an outfit she turned the hanger toward the open room. After six months or a year, any clothing on hangers still facing the wall was eligible for giving away.

Principles for evaluating your clothes:

- If you have enough money to buy any clothes you want and the room to store them, it doesn't mean you *have* to. Give some of that money to those who don't have the luxury of wearing something new.

- Look for quality and buy from local merchants, even if it costs a little more. It should last longer and will support the local economy.
- Don't be a slave to fashion trends. Make your own unique fashion statement by buying or making what *you* like.

You might have a different strategy for pruning clothes and other items around the house, but I hope my experience at least inspires you to evaluate how letting go of some clothing will lighten your life and give you more space. After two years, I'm now on my second round of thinning my clothes, and I've been surprised that items I resisted giving away the first time now seem totally dispensable. I guess I just needed time to grieve their going. The lesson is that not everything has to go at once. Making the first cut was habit-forming for me, and now I evaluate what to keep by only hanging on to clothes that I absolutely love and letting go of the rest. It's an ongoing process.

Books, Games, and Electronics

I put books, games, and electronics under the über category of entertainment or communication since it includes old-fashioned paper books, board games, and the endless supply of communication devices and accessories. Each of these categories was difficult for me to get a handle on, but for different reasons—books because we had over 1,339 of them; games because they carried childhood attachments, and electronics because I didn't understand what was still useful and what was obsolete.

As I was struggling to decide which books to keep and which to give away, one young adult quipped, "Give them all away, then buy any you really want for an e-reader." I kept professional books, theology books (they never become obsolete), repair books, and much-loved children's books. I finally settled on the following as criteria to use when evaluating which books to give away:

- novels that I'll never read again
- text books from college and grad school
- books that contained information I can now more easily get online

Games such as Candy Land, Monopoly, and Parcheesi became a tortuous decision because they all held fond memories of family game playing. I invoked the "Grandchildren and Others May Visit" rule for many of these. Adult games like Scrabble, Settlers of Catan, and Carcassonne were easy because we still play them. But there were still about thirty games and puzzles remaining. I gave away half.

Electronics required the assistance of an expert—at least someone much younger than me. I called in our one local son who advised which computers, printers, phones, and cords were worth keeping. Where to responsibly dispose of broken or outdated electronics is covered in chapter 9, Waste Less—Save More Energy, and in the appendix.

Everything Else

Everything else is a pretty big category. It includes bedding, bathroom stuff, sports equipment, arts and crafts, knickknacks, holiday supplies, tools, garage stuff, and kitchen equipment—pretty much everything *but* the kitchen sink. The principles we've been talking about with clothes, books, and electronics still apply. I looked over what I had, decided what I still used, and put the things I was willing to part with in an empty corner of the house until I could efficiently take it to a new home. There were some items, however, that defied standard categories. I think you might get a kick out of them.

- Dead pets: We have been pet-free for a number of years, so I was surprised to find dog supplies, bird, hamster, rabbit, and lizard cages, and other paraphernalia for pets that died a long time ago.

- Past pests: I fancy myself a fairly ecological home owner, but when it comes to insects and deer invading my garden, it's war! After carefully planting and cultivating my garden all spring, I was not going to cede it to hungry bugs and other critters. Recently I have discovered several nontoxic ways to control these pests, yet I still had quite a stash of toxic chemicals in a cupboard. These aren't easy to dispose of responsibly. Once a year our county offers a hazardous waste drop-off service. There was one pesticide that even *they* wouldn't take. I decided to pour it on a stand of poison ivy behind our house. It was a win/win solution.

First Steps and Big Steps

Light and easy

For beginners or those fearful of sort-and-pitch, consider starting with a messy or stuffed drawer. You may discover that once you have experienced that first neat drawer, you'll be compelled to keep going. If not, that's fine; at least you have one cleaner space in your home.

Pace yourself. Throw away what's broken, give away what you don't need, or find a better place for odds and ends that don't belong in the drawer. Eventually graduate to another relatively easy category of stuff to go through.

Extreme lightness

Pick a room or a closet. Devote a day or a weekend to organizing, repairing, and releasing its treasures. An alternative is to pick a length of time—the forty days of Lent, a particular month, or a two- or three-day period and commit to selecting at least one thing each day to give away.

Extreme, extreme lightness may mean you consider downsizing your home, not just the stuff in it. This isn't something you decide in a day or a week; but you come to it over weeks or months of other lightening work. By the time you have pondered and sorted your way through every room, you will develop a stronger idea of what is truly important to your living space, and this may lead to the larger decision of keeping the present house or finding something more suited to your present life.

For Meditation

Jesus, looking at [the rich young man], loved him and said, "You lack one thing; go, sell what you own, and give the money to the poor, and you will have treasure in heaven; then come, follow me." When he heard this, he was shocked and went away grieving, for he had many possessions.

—Mark 10:21–22

For Reflection or Discussion

- What would be the easiest material possession for me to give away?
- What would be the hardest material possession for me to give away?
- Do I have a system for giving stuff away or a regular place to which I can take clothing, furniture, etc.?
- Books and electronics are often harder to give away than clothes. What criteria would I use for keeping books? How do I decide when a TV, computer, or phone has become obsolete for me but still might be useful to someone else?

6

Carry Less—Move More Lightly

For me it's all about finding the perfect purse. It must be small, light, versatile, and carry everything I need. I'm not sure what the male equivalent would be.

The catch in my perfect purse search is "everything I need." When going to the corner store, all I really need is money and my driver's license (maybe not even the license if it really is the corner store and I'm walking). When going to work or a meeting, I also need a pen, planner, comb, and perhaps the cell phone. (Others may be able to delete the planner because their calendar, notes, and contacts are all on their smart phone.) When traveling a distance, I need clothes, toiletries, and a whole bunch more. In my never-ending quest to carry less, I've found that a lot depends on where I'm going and what stage of life I'm in.

But why do I even care about carrying less, and does it really simplify my life or just leave me less prepared for any needs that may come up? First, I admit that I have a personality quirk that gives me great pleasure in seeing how little I can carry with me and still have "enough." I love small things and enjoy miniaturizing whatever I can. Second, I have a bad back. Physically, I know I'll need to visit my friendly chiropractor if I carry or lift something too heavy. But mostly, as I've learned to whittle down what I carry, I've found freedom in being able to move more lightly and swiftly. I can go farther and longer without getting tired. I also don't lose as much because there's not so much to keep track of. I don't worry much about things being stolen since what I'm carrying is compact and close to my body. Following are some things I've learned about carrying less.

Connecting to Your Stage of Life
For those in the first half of life

Carrying less on your back or shoulder might not be so difficult for those whose lives can be contained in a slim smart phone. Here, the challenge may be to evaluate how we use our convenient electronic personal assistants. Does it distract me from the physical presence of those humans near me? Is it so important that I would be lost without it (virtually, emotionally, or geographically)?

Of course if you're a parent, there's all the paraphernalia that goes along with carting children from place to place. It's hard to streamline that too much because kids' needs are not entirely predictable.

Perhaps the bigger challenge to younger adults is not how much physical stuff to carry, but how much does my concern about success, my appearance, and making money weigh me down?

For those in the second half of life

Carrying less may be a physical necessity due to aging backs, but it may also mean we're figuring out what's really important to keep near at hand. During the active parenting phase of life, you may have needed diaper bags, forgotten school supplies, and tissues for wiping up spills and tears. Now you may need only the tissues.

But then, because we *are* more experienced in what needs may pop up on a shopping trip or when traveling a distance, it's easy to think we need to carry everything but the kitchen sink. It is possible to be over prepared and wear out our energy because we're carrying so much stuff.

Carry Less around Town

During my year of giveaways, I eventually examined what I stored under our bed. (Beds are a nice hiding place because things can stay there a mighty long time without being noticed or causing trouble—sort of like quiet kids.) I was surprised to find a stash of old purses. Obviously I wasn't using them. A couple of them were of the elegant evening-bag variety. I gave all of them away and never looked back. The challenge was to come up with an all-purpose purse or two so I wouldn't have to keep transferring the contents from one purse to another. But first I had to identify what my real needs were.

When traveling around town, I've pared my usual needs down to

- Cash
- Driver's license; credit, bank, insurance, and library cards
- Photos of our children
- Cell phone
- Comb
- Teeny tiny notebook with pen
- Teeny tiny flashlight
- Teeny tiny rain cap (folded to 3 inches)
- Glasses (When I'm wearing my contacts, I can skip these.)
- Keys, which hang on a clip outside the purse

This all fits into a small black bag that hangs on a strap crossing my body. My current bag has a satiny finish that in my opinion makes it look like it could be appropriate for either dressy or casual wear. Of course my standards aren't too high. (Lowering standards is another strategy for getting along with less.) For the male perspective, my husband can go with even less (just his wallet) since he always wears his glasses, the cell phone is in another pocket, his hair doesn't require protection from the rain, and he asks me for pen and paper if he needs to write something down.

When we are traveling to a job or meeting, packing gets more complicated for both of us. I have a larger bag which can fit file folders, my planner, a netbook computer, a mini-Bible, a variety of writing implements and presentation supplies, basic cosmetics and toiletries, plus mini-headphones for airplane movies. This standard equipment stays in the "big purse" all the time and then I just slip my small bag into it too. My husband uses his backpack for the same contents, minus the cosmetics. When I'm giving a workshop, however, I have to schlep along a CD player (have not yet graduated to a tiny MP3 player and tiny plug-in speaker) and a roller bag full of books and other supplies. It reminds me of the days I was transporting kids except that then I didn't get paid for all the stuff I was carting around.

Carry Less on Long Hauls

For out-of-town travel, here are some things I've learned from years of traveling by car and plane to a variety of environments, some of them in developing countries. It might seem counterintuitive to say that carrying less makes a trip more enjoyable, since you might not have a particular convenience (or necessity) that would make the trip more comfortable. Assuming that you have the basics, however, much of the other stuff can just weigh you down and interfere with the freedom to explore and interact with people from different backgrounds.

I have learned that it's possible to fly anywhere for up to two months with only a carry-on (and a husband to lift things). Not only is it easier to transport from place to place but it also avoids lost luggage, and my frugal side is happy not to pay to check a bag. I have to break some of my frugal rules and buy small specialized items of clothing or toiletries, but it's worth it to me. Also:

- Cultivate "easy hair," i.e., very short or very long.
- Pack for one week, i.e., eight underpants/socks and several versatile outfits. (Plan to wash clothes once a week.)
- Ideally, take everything in one carry-on that rolls, plus a backpack/large purse.
- Wear your heaviest/bulkiest items, such as your coat.
- Preferably plan your trip for warm weather so you don't need heavy clothes.

- Use scarves instead of heavy jewelry. They're light and can make one basic outfit look like four.

- Avoid umbrellas and simply take a fold-up rain hat or rainproof jacket with a hood.

- Color coordinate your wardrobe so that most everything goes with each other.

- Try to limit shoes to two pair: one for heavy-duty walking (these are the ones to wear on the plane) and another that are still comfortable but dressier, such as sandals. Please note: Unless you can walk comfortably forever in flip-flops, it's not worth the thirty seconds you save at airport security.

- Duct tape. It can fix just about anything.

I confess, packing lightly is a hobby for me bordering on an obsession. The specifics may not fit your personality, but the larger point is to focus on the people you encounter in travel. Being burdened by baggage can rob us of the pleasure of surprises and the challenge of having to rely on others. Sometimes we will need a Good Samaritan. Sometimes we will *be* the Good Samaritan. Moving more lightly has allowed me to go off the beaten path and learn that strangers are almost always happy to help when approached with respect and humility. It's worth the risk. It's helpful to have a buddy. Jesus sent the apostles out in pairs for a reason (Mark 6:7).

First Steps and Big Steps

Light and easy

Start by making a list of what daily necessities you need when you leave your home. Add a few things that will help you feel prepared for an emergency. Figure out the best way to carry your necessities. Perhaps you've already accomplished this physical step. If so, focus on unrealistic expectations for yourself that you might be carrying. Can you let go of one?

Extreme lightness

The most extreme challenge will not be reducing the physical things you carry; that can be fun, even entertaining. The deeper challenge will be to let go of pride in reducing your baggage. Bragging about how little you pack will not earn you frequent flyer miles but only increase your obnoxiousness. Extreme lightness also involves knowing when to carry less emotional baggage and let go of thinking you have to solve other people's problems. More on this in the next chapter.

For Meditation

He ordered them to take nothing for their journey except a staff; no bread, no bag, no money in their belts; but to wear sandals and not to put on two tunics.

—Mark 6:8–9

For Reflection or Discussion

- Jesus was preparing his disciples to go out in pairs to preach the good news. How literally do I read the above Scripture for my daily life? What is the message behind the specifics?

- What necessities do I typically carry when I leave home? Are there any adjustments I'd like to make in what or how much I carry?

- Do I tend to be the kind of person who is ready for any emergency, or do I prefer not to be bogged down with supplies? Do I know some people of both types? What are the pros and cons of each approach?

- What surprising or difficult experiences have I had when traveling away from home? How have they enriched me? How have they upset or challenged me?

7

Weighed Down by Other People's Stuff

"Dad, I hope you still have that heavy winter jacket of mine. No, I don't need it now. It's always 80+ degrees here in Singapore, but I'll need it when I come home to visit over Christmas."

—Aaron

"No, you can't give away all my role-playing game figurines and books. It's not that I need them now but they're keepsakes."
—Dacian, who lives about a mile away in a tiny apartment

Our daughter, Heidi, who was living in Afghanistan, said she had no use for sterling silver there, but asked me to save the family heirlooms for her because she would like them eventually.

Not all the stuff that resides in our homes is ours to give away. It gets a little dicey when trying to decide for another person what is worth keeping or discarding. Other stuff that can weigh a person down includes our adult children's belongings and other supplies that we may have agreed to store for friends or organizations. There can also be emotional baggage we carry, such as problems that others expect us to solve ("If you invite that bum to Christmas dinner, I'm not coming"). This chapter will address primarily the material stuff. I'll focus on emotional baggage in chapter 10, "Hurry and Worry Less."

Connecting to Your Stage of Life
For those in the first half of life
People in the first half of life probably don't have a lot of stuff they're saving for other people. It's possible, however, that your parents are offering you used furniture or other household items. These may be welcome or they may not be your style. Saying no graciously can be tricky. If you really can't use the items, try offering them to other siblings or to those in greater need than yourself.

For those in the second half of life
You will probably be able to identify with much of this chapter's content. Deciding when to be the family storage shed and when to say, "If you don't take it with you the next time you're home, it's history" is also a tricky decision.

Let Go of Adult Children's Stuff
When trying to clean out their young adults' leftovers, other parents often tell me of the eminently reasonable strategy that they use: "Come and get it by _____, or I'm giving it away."

This makes a lot of sense for most parents. But two of our four children live in other countries with the hope of sometime returning to the USA. One child lives in a studio apartment and barely has room for his two most important possessions: his computer and minimalist clothes. One child is married, has kids and a small house, but both spouses brought significant possessions to the marriage. Their storage space is already filled to the max.

Then there's also the ever-present "Grandparent Clause." In the back of my mind looms the thought that even offspring who don't seem inclined to start a family in the near future might someday have a baby. Having inherited the Vogt thrift and low-income genes, they may really appreciate baby items that we've saved. Surely, they would want those adorable Polly Flinders dresses or at least a few extra spit-up cloths. And of course we need to have toys for the little ones to play with when they come to visit. I know this "Grandparent Clause" might violate Rule of Thumb #5: If I don't need it now (or soon), give it to someone who does. But there are exceptions to every rule.

Because of these exceptions, I used the following process when deciding what and how to deal with our adult children's belongings that were stored in our home.

1. Gather each child's stuff to inventory and sort according to three broad categories:

   – No Brainer items that surely our sons or daughter would not mind giving away
   – Parental Attachment items that I didn't want to give away for sentimental reasons
   – Questionable items

2. Seek permission.

   I then asked if anyone objected to my giving away the No Brainer items and what they wanted to keep from the Questionable category. I thought the easiest child would be the local one, who has always been a minimalist (I thought). He came over to the house to review the proposed giveaways and proclaimed: "This silly give-away project of yours is jeopardizing my home storage vault. No, you cannot sell my old adventure fantasy books to the used book store. I don't care that it could make me some money." He released about one third of the items for disposal and I packed the rest into a small trunk. Which brings me to . . .

3. Have a container.

   It doesn't have to be a trunk, but these are convenient because they double as seats or tables. One child has a closet shelf. Another has an old desk that we use for company but the drawers have his treasures in them.

4. Cut some slack.

Although ideally we would have four small trunks, each neatly holding mementos waiting for our kids to claim when they come of age, our kids are more than "of age" right now, and we're still negotiating. Our daughter learned of a skirt that I was giving away from seeing a photo of it on my blog. She quickly e-mailed me, saying she liked that skirt and if I still had it to please save it for her. Of course it wasn't her skirt to begin with, but we're about the same size so I recaptured it from my "give-away corner," and it now awaits her return.

Even the best laid plans can backfire. Family Systems Theory and life experience have taught me that when one person in a family takes on a mission, no matter how laudatory, it will backfire unless it has the cooperation of those living in the home. My grand plan of clearing our house of stuff I no longer needed made ripples in the lives of those who left home but still consider our home their personal storage unit. I've bent. They've bent. I'm trying to be as flexible as a pipe cleaner. I guess it relates to the spiritual principle: Control people less—love and free people more.

To Keep or Not to Keep— Other People's Stuff

Since we have a relatively large house (an advantage when we had four children at home but it has lots of free space now that we don't), it is the logical place for friends or relatives in transition to store their stuff. I consider this a ministry, and so it doesn't violate my "Live More Lightly" creed. If it lightens someone else's life to keep dressers, beds, tables, and family heirlooms at our place—at least for a while—that's fine. There's a corner of the basement for that, and as long as the basement stays dry, all is good. Some people have died before they've claimed their stuff. Then it goes to a better, higher place, just like them—at least a place that no longer causes us to worry about basement leaks.

Volunteer organizations often have supplies, archives, and inventory that need a home. Certainly this is an entirely optional decision when deciding whether to offer your home as the landing place, if only for a while.

Currently we're storing archived papers from one forty-year-old organization. As long as the papers are happy on a top closet shelf and no one's asking for us to retrieve information from them, it's not harming anyone. Of course, the conscientious archivist would make sure it's on acid-free paper (it isn't), and ideally all information would be transferred to a digital format. This would be both time-consuming and expensive. **Rule of Thumb #7 applies here: Decide which technologies save you time, energy, and money—and which ones waste time, energy, and money**. Sometimes we have to make judicious decisions about what's worth our time. If this organization ever finds a compulsive, techno-wizard member with a lot of extra time, we have several storage boxes to transfer.

A more fun but frightening storage request we had was to house a five-foot-tall papier-mâché pig. I thought it was a fun conversation piece, but a couple of youngsters who visited found it intimidating. We eventually passed the fun on to another family.

The kind of "other people's stuff" that is not really a burden has to do with stuff people give us to pass on to other worthy places. Our home seems to have developed a reputation as a "go to place" for neighbors to drop off their gently used clothes and gear to be recycled. It's taken awhile to learn about our community's recycling/reusing resources, so I'm happy to provide this service.

Let Go of Other People's Problems

It's generous and a good use of space to store other people's stuff if they need it and if you have the space. It's much riskier, and often inappropriate, to take on other people's problems. Offer a listening ear and compassion. If you have the resources and time to help without enabling, that's wonderful. But there comes a point in many good-hearted helpers' lives when they realize that the help-ee's problems are unduly weighing them down and beyond their ability to fix. Sometimes it's the right time to stretch your own resources to help, but other times your help can get in the way of people stretching and learning to solve their own problems.

Apprising an adult child of reputable counselors or programs for her troubled marriage may help. Making the appointment is being over-responsible. Giving financial assistance to a friend to finish his education so he can get a better job can help. Paying off his debts just delays the day of reckoning. Let go of carrying another person's troubled baggage by giving them a rolling suitcase, not by carrying it yourself. Don't get in the middle of another's relationship problems—that's called triangulation. Better to give tools for creating the solution than to hand over the solution. If your overly soft heart is causing you angst, stiffen your resolve by remembering the flight attendant's safety instructions, "Put your own oxygen mask on first or you won't be able to help anyone else."

First Steps and Big Steps

Light and easy

If you don't have much room, you have an easy out. "Sorry, we just don't have room." If you're storing adult children's stuff, I recommend the conventional approach, "Come and get it by _____, or I'm giving it away."

Extreme lightness

You can always do what one friend did. "Beloved adult son, we're moving to another state and just can't take it (or you) with us." This applied to a son who needed to get out of the house and make a life of his own.

For Meditation

Perform all thy actions with mind concentrated on the Divine, renouncing attachment and looking upon success and failure with an equal eye. Spirituality implies equanimity.

—Bhagavad Gita

For Reflection or Discussion

- How do I clear my life of other people's stuff?
- When do I know that I have taken on other people's problems?
- Have I ever been the one in transition who needed a place to store stuff? How did I feel about asking for help?
- Where do I draw the line between keeping family heirlooms or adult children's belongings versus just clearing it out? Have I determined a statute of limitation on how long I should keep others' stuff?

8

Dealing with Intangibles

I had just finished typing a complicated report on the computer when, in a moment of distraction, I forgot to save it. Aarrgh! I know there are probably ways to retrieve my work and that Jesus saves, but I didn't.

It's going to take time or a visit from my son to figure this out. It's not life threatening. It's only words, but it does take time. As another son reminds me, "Time is money."

As difficult as it may be to let go of extra clothes, tools, or other material possessions, the intangible stuff of our lives is even trickier to get a grip on. Intangibles include:

- Information (and all the technology we use to gather, share, and store it)
- Relationships
- The Familiar (places, jobs, habits)
- Memories

Many intangibles fill our lives with joy; for instance, we can communicate with faraway loved ones through the Internet. Other intangibles complicate and clutter our lives like spending way too much time on social media or brooding over a lost relationship. Here, we'll consider how less information, efficiency, and memorabilia can be freeing and when it's just foolish not to take advantage of virtual tools. Sometimes letting go of a relationship or habit makes room for better things, but other times it's a sad loss. How do we know when to let go and when to hold on to things we can't touch?

Connecting to Your Stage of Life
For those in the first half of life

Intangibles may lure you into letting the latest technology preempt your human relationships and gobble up any discretionary money. Be willing to share your natural expertise (without being condescending) with those who don't know the difference between a browser and a search engine. Instead of just adding new gadgets to your repertoire, figure out how to use technology to simplify your electronic life rather than be a slave to cords and chargers.

You may also be in a time of life when moving and changing jobs is par for the course. Letting go of familiar surroundings and people is an emotional challenge, but then technology can keep you connected. Remember the spiritual principle: People are more important than things.

For those in the second half of life

You, like me, have probably ventured into the Internet world of e-mail and social networking. Perhaps it is thrilling or simply unfathomable. This chapter will explore ways to keep in touch without becoming overwhelmed with technology that changes before you have the last update mastered.

You may be wondering how long (or if) to hang on to those old photo albums and when to toss your children's art projects from grade school. Remember that the wisdom you've gained over years of watching fads come and go can give you perspective on what's really important. It's not how fast you can do something or how many Facebook friends you have, but the quality of your presence to others.

Information

I thought I was doing pretty well in pruning my possessions until I got to my computer. I started to realize that probably my biggest intangible burden in our tech-heavy culture is TMI: Too Much Information. It was a daunting task to determine which information was worth consuming and which gadgets best helped me consume it—in ways that didn't burden me with trivia or the weight of the world. It may seem contradictory but the more I upgraded my computer or phone, the more lost I became. I keep telling myself that eventually all this information processing and faster communication is going to simplify my life, but there's a big learning curve and sometimes it gets harder before it gets better. I'm in the process of discerning my own point of diminishing returns whereby more information does not bring more ease or quality of life. "You got to know when to hold 'em and know when to fold 'em" and let go. It's a very personal decision.

In regard to technology, although I'm not a techno-peasant, neither am I a techno-wizard. I have a Web site and a blog. I receive about seventy-five e-mails a day, check into Facebook, Twitter, and LinkedIn. I read two daily newspapers, various periodicals, and am a devoted listener of National Public Radio. I get a lot of good information, but acquiring it can become time-consuming and overwhelming.

Sometimes less technology has humanized my life and made it simpler. Sometimes more technology has helped me to stay connected to people and to accomplish more, even though it has also complicated my life. Here are some questions to consider, followed by ways I've tried to tame the flood of information.

TV/Radio/Movies

Which of these media are time hogs and which can be used while multitasking? TV was an easy one because most commercial programs were time hogs for me. I gave away one TV and limit my watching to one favorite regular show. (Full disclosure: I make exceptions for things like the Olympics, breaking news, and being sick.) A couple of other programs I watch online at my convenience while exercising. I can multitask by dressing, driving, gardening, or walking while listening to public radio—thus no extra time spent. Consider these media conquered.

Cell Phones

When does a cell phone save time, promote safety, and simplify your life, and when does it just eat up money and interrupt your focus on the person in front of you? We gave away older phones during my give-away year, but we have accepted that having a cell phone is a modern necessity.

Since both Jim and I work at home, we decided to have only one cell phone and it's not very smart. I know people who have no cell phone (most of them are over eighty or hermits), and I know people who have more than one (a personal one and a work one). I've seen how cell phones simplify and enhance our kids' lives. (Once our grand-child was sick. Soon after our daughter-in-law dropped him off to the nanny, the nanny sent a photo to her phone showing how the baby was sleeping peacefully. What a smart nanny and a relief to a worried par-ent.) Having a cell phone has simplified my life when traveling, shop-ping, and in emergencies.

As our son, Aaron, puts it, "Having a smart phone has made my life much easier. However, I have to be disciplined about putting meet-ings into the calendar and keeping my contacts up-to-date. It sim-plifies my life to have everything in one device: phone, e-mail, Web browser, camera, video recorder, music player, data storage, gaming device, movie player, PowerPoint presentation remote, flashlight, and alarm clock. Since such phones can get quite expensive, it took a fair bit of research to make sure that I got a quality product that was a good fit for me. Of course, nothing stays current for long these days. Soon, an updated gadget surfaces and then I have to evaluate whether it's worth an upgrade."

In addition to researching the best deals, another complication is learning how to use all the functions. For these reasons we're sticking with a basic phone/camera version for now. It's simpler. Several rules of thumb that have proven to tame cell phone mania for me are:

- The live person in front of me always trumps virtual communication unless it's an emergency.

- Just because it rings doesn't mean I have to answer.

- Speaking of rings, less noise is better; cell phones should be kept in a pocket and on vibrate.

Computers and the Internet

Which elements of the Internet save you time and which waste it? Here it's good to apply Rule of Thumb #7: Decide which technologies save time, energy, and money—and which ones waste time, energy, and money. As a writer and mega-volunteer who works out of my home, I spend a lot of time with my computer. I remember the days of sending out newsletters as bulk mailings, waiting several days to get a phone call returned, or allowing a week to receive a response to a snail mail letter. It was time-consuming, expensive, and inefficient. Now I can send an e-mail blast to thousands of recipients all over the world in a matter of minutes. More technology has allowed me to do more in less time. It has saved me time and money, and allowed me to be more productive. So, what's not to love?

Not only do I send out a lot of e-mails, I also get a glut of them. Regarding Internet use, being "blessed by less" has meant learning how to filter, file, and delete. The Internet can be my friend but it must be a disciplined friend, and that discipline comes from me. Some rules I've developed for myself are:

- Have folders to organize incoming information.

- Check Facebook daily but limit the amount of time spent.

- Don't bother trying to build up a lot of Twitter followers. Many people who have thousands of followers got them artificially through automated programs.

- Don't waste time playing Internet games or surfing the net for recreation. I'd rather do live recreation.
- I sign petitions that I agree with, but seldom post them to Facebook or forward them to others to clutter their inboxes.
- Be cautious of e-mails with vague subject lines.
- Occasionally, when on vacation or retreat, I've fasted from the Internet. This sounds like a great idea, but I seldom last longer than a couple of days since it complicates my life when I have to catch up on all those new e-mails when I get home.
- Virus protection is worth it.

Of course there are those days when the Internet gods are playing in the clouds and messing up my virtual world. This is when I rue my limited technological skills. Ignorance is not bliss and less is not more when I need competent tech support. Having spent way too many hours trying to unravel an Internet glitch by myself or with people in far-off lands (once I've finally gotten through to a tech support person), I've learned that it lightens my mind and saves hours of work to pay for off-site back-up help.

GPS Devices and Maps

Is auto travel a Christopher Columbus type of adventure for you, or do you mainly want to get to your destination without getting lost? Being directionally challenged, one of the great additions to my driving life has been the GPS my kids gave me for Christmas. Yes, this is an additional informational gadget, but it has lifted worry and stress from my driving. I put it on mute so there's less noise.

Technology can both simplify and complicate our lives. When it deepens my relationship with other human beings and my spiritual life, it is of God and is a blessing. When it robs me of giving attention to the people I love and who depend on me, it is a curse. To avoid overdoing it, I've found it useful to be almost the last kid on my block to get the latest technology. By the time I do buy a new gadget or program, the experts have had time to work out the bugs and glitches. I benefit from other people's experience, the prices have usually come down, and I don't have to learn as many iterations of new formats.

Although so much information in today's culture is conveyed through technology, I would be remiss not to say a word about being wordy. One thing I've learned as a writer and a parent is that some people talk too much and others not enough. Most people err on the side of too much. When I started to give things away, I didn't realize that this practice might include pruning my words. I lean toward being an extrovert, which means that I talk in order to think. It's also easier for me to write long than write short. If you are the opposite, then your challenge probably is to be willing to share ideas, feelings, and to be vulnerable. For us extroverts, it means we need the self-discipline to stop talking and be more concise. This is especially important for parenting and in group discussions. Fewer and more well-chosen words can make a stronger statement. This is especially true when it comes to complaints and criticisms. This brings us to relationships.

Relationships

People are intangibles because they are moving targets. They grow and move. We aspire to love our parents and children forever, but there comes a time when we must let go—a loved one dies, a child gets married or otherwise sets off on her own path. Our hearts may always be attached, but we lose direct control over these lives, and that is good. Parents tell me that the most freeing advice I give in my workshops is this: *Parents are responsible for the process of bringing up children; parents are not responsible for the outcome.* Let go of guilt and pointless attempts at control.

But letting go of control of our children doesn't mean that all our responsibility is ended. In the case of minors, we still need to feed, clothe, house, and educate them. Yet, the truly responsible parent pays attention to whether too much time at a paying job is starting to interfere with paying attention to the important people in our lives. Giving our children guidance and inspiration cannot always be done in absentia. To discern this balance involves having a clear vision of how much income your family needs to lead a satisfying life. It sometimes means trading income for relationship time. Discerning that takes authentic self-knowledge and family consultation.

Adult children also deserve our ongoing love but not necessarily our financial support. At their stage of life, letting go of parental control often means not confusing our dreams for their success with our young adult's freedom to make mistakes. Advice, when requested, is fine but let go of managing their future.

When our children were young, my husband and I chose to have only one full-time job between us in order to have a parent at home with the kids most of the time. This meant that our standard of living had to decrease during those years. This didn't always go over well with our kids, especially as they merged into the teen years and complained that they'd be fine with our working outside the home more if it meant we could buy more stuff. In revisiting this issue with our young adults, however, they admitted that our way was probably worth it and that they would also sacrifice some income for more time with the people they love. Of course some careers don't lend themselves to part-time or delayed entry jobs. And many people must take whatever jobs they can. But sometimes simply being open to adjustments for the sake of relationships can make it easier to see alternatives.

Letting our adult children choose their own paths has been a bittersweet experience. During their teen years we gladly encouraged them to take part in international exchange programs. After college, each young adult did a year or two of service, most often in an international setting. We were proud of them and even fantasized that they might meet the love of their life among their volunteer colleagues. What we didn't anticipate was that these international forays might become long-lasting stays, or that the love of their life might hail from a country clear across the globe. Currently, our family is spread over three continents.

Meanwhile our neighbor has two young adults and they both live within a couple of blocks. They "get to do" primary or back-up grandchild care. They are lucky. I miss not having our children closer, especially the grandchildren, but we do keep in touch virtually. We put the money we save by living lightly toward trips to visit our children, who believed us when we said, "There's a big world out there. Experience it." I've had to let go of the dream of having all our kids nearby and have replaced it with knowing they are independent, loving people who are finding their own course to happiness.

Beyond family members, good friends move away, sweethearts find someone else, we change jobs, or our values may no longer be in sync with those we used to spend time with. Letting go of a relationship does not mean forgetting about the happy times or goodness of the person, but letting go of thinking we have control over others or that they belong to us. Facebook, e-mail, and Twitter notwithstanding, research suggests that most humans can only sustain about 150 meaningful relationships at one time. Don't feel guilty about not keeping up with everyone you've ever known. Gently let them go, or send them an annual family letter.

The Familiar

Letting go of the familiar is easy for some but becomes harder for most of us as we age. If you're the adventurous, risk-taking type who likes to change your Facebook photo every week, this is probably not

a problem for you. For the rest of us, letting go of familiar surroundings and ways of doing things can be unsettling and often painful. Like
most people, I've changed cities, jobs, homes, and family roles. Getting
married and having children were happy transitions but still stressful.
The scarier transitions were job loss and relocation.

Beyond these big life changes, however, are many tinier changes
that can interrupt our lives and knock us off balance for a while. As
I was busy getting rid of material stuff in my home, I was surprised
that changing the e-mail address that I'd had for about fifteen years
felt more disruptive than giving away clothes. First I spent hours with
tech support figuring out the intricacies of how to seamlessly forward
e-mails sent to my previous address. Then I had to learn a whole new
process for doing things that had become second nature under the previous e-mail system. This adjustment also happens when I update a
computer program or cell phone, and when we changed from VCR
tapes to DVDs. (Please don't tell me we're going to replace DVDs with
something else!) It took time to navigate the changes, but my online
life is easier now that I've let go of an old way.

It's even harder to let go of bad habits, which are simply familiar
patterns that stick because we keep repeating them and get some kind
of pleasure out of them. For example, during Lent I decided to give up
complaining. I figured this would cost no money, take no time, and
make me a kinder, holier person to be around. It was simply a matter
of saying fewer complaining words. It was only when I became more
conscious of this bad habit that I realized how much I complained and
how difficult it would be to stop. I got better, but maintained my san-
ity only by declaring that because Sundays were not officially Lenten
days that I would allow myself one Sunday complaint. I also invented
a new category of speech entitled "venting." Under this term I allowed
myself occasionally to vent to my husband lest an irritation build up to

the point of making me feel angry. His job was to stop me if it crossed over into the realm of complaining. He was generous.

So, how has letting go of familiar things and bad habits blessed my life? Letting go of a city or job whose time had come forced me to stretch my vision and try new things. Letting go of familiar technology forced me to learn better ways of using improved technology. Letting go of a bad habit helped me to become a more positive person to be around. Even though stripping away the old and familiar can be painful, it often has to go to make room for something new and creative.

Memories

Some of the hardest things to let go of are memories. In fact, maybe we shouldn't. Certainly memories are precious reminders of people and experiences that live in our minds and can inspire us into the future. Although we can't physically touch a memory, still I had many material reminders of happy memories. Memorabilia such as photos, trophies, and souvenirs were tucked away in albums, trunks, and bookshelves. Would it dishonor the people to let go of their gifts? Would I lose memory of the past if I let go of the photos? What about future generations who want to see what their great-grandparents looked like? What about those trophies that remind me of our kids' childhood accomplishments?

The ideal solution would be to scan all the photos into a digital format, take photos of the trophies and let a scout troop or school repurpose them, and display the best of the international souvenirs. It's times like these that a conscientious minimalist has to make some hard decisions about how to honor the past without eating up undue time in the present.

I knew that digitalizing ten photo albums dating back to 1950 would take way more time and money than I wanted to spend. I decided to store them until one of the kids wants to take on this project. Photos from the past ten years are all digital ones. I gave half the trophies away and am still looking for that scout troop. Some of the souvenirs are displayed but others I gave away. I honor them by taking a photo (digital of course) and giving them away or recycling. I deal with clothing that has sentimental value by wearing it one last time with mindfulness and then giving it away.

First Steps and Big Steps

Light and easy

Try a "tech fast" for a day, or longer. Spend the time you would have used online to be present to a loved one, face-to-face.

Is there one bad habit you'd like to let go of? Perhaps eating a particular junk food, watching too much TV, wasting time on social media, or not flossing? Try changing it for a week or more. See if it sticks.

Extreme lightness

If you have been avoiding the Internet or social media because it's intimidating, take a risk. Invite someone younger to tutor you, and learn a new skill. Consider it bonding time even if you don't use it much. If, on the other hand, you and your electronic gadgets are inseparable, honestly take stock of how you can tame your dependence. Log how much time you spend on TV, videos, or social media for purely recreational purposes. You don't have to go cold turkey; decide how to bring a human balance to your life.

If this is too threatening, you can substitute going through all your old memorabilia and convert them to a digital format.

For Meditation

And after he had dismissed the crowds, he went up the mountain by himself to pray.

—Matthew 14:23

For Reflection or Discussion

- Do I have enough quiet and solitude in my life? How might I get it if I need more?

- Which would be the hardest intangible for me to let go of: information (including technology), people, familiar places and ways of doing things, memorabilia?

- What step could I take to tame too much information, to let go of trying to control other people, or to break a bad habit?

- In regard to memorabilia, one thing I definitely want to keep because it feeds my soul is _____. One thing I could rather easily let go of is _____.

9

Waste Less—Save More Energy

I went to a charitable event the other night and found myself grumbling about the hosts' use of bottled water instead of just having pitchers of water. I smugly picked up a Styrofoam cup meant for coffee and filled it from the drinking fountain. My companion pointed out that at least the water bottle could be recycled while the Styrofoam could not. It's complicated.

Many of the daily decisions we consider about saving and wasting stuff can be argued several ways. Is it better to buy an expensive electric car, thus producing less carbon emissions, or is it better to just drive less or to move closer to my work? What kind of energy is being used to produce the electricity for the electric car? Is it even a practical choice to move or can I afford a more expensive car? What about all the time it would take to research these complicated questions? I won't fault you if you say, "Hey, I've got diapers to change or a sick child to care for. I have other priorities right now." Yes, it's complicated, but nearly always there's something you can do.

In the case of the bottled water at the public event, I decided to take a small, first step. The next week, I offered to bring several pitchers from home and filled them with tap water at the site. I also brought recyclable cups. The ideal would be to have glasses that could then be washed by hand or in a dishwasher, but that would take extra time by the volunteer leaders or electricity to run the dishwasher. (Actually, I took the plastic cups home and ran them through our dishwasher to be reused the next week. It wasn't a huge crowd.) Not a perfect solution, but it's a start. And I tried to do it with a smile, not a smug look.

How much you choose to do in a given situation could depend on what stage of life you are in and on what else makes demands on your time.

During my intensive give-away year, I eventually realized that choosing what to give away was relatively easy compared to deciding where to take it. For a while I stored much of the stuff in a corner of our house while I considered and researched where to take it all. As I reflected on what to do with this stuff, I realized that I was also using a lot of my personal energy, i.e. time, and wasting the earth's energy, i.e. fossil fuels, at the same time I was trying to do good. I also noticed not just what I gave away but what I threw away. As environmental activist Julia Butterfly Hill says, "When you say you are going to throw something away, where's 'away'?" It's always somewhere. This leads me to three dimensions of wasting less: stuff, energy, and garbage.

Connecting to Your Stage of Life

For those in the first half of life

In a household with kids, there are limits on both time and money. To avoid becoming a frazzled parent, you may decide that convenience is the better part of valor. You might opt for shortcuts such as convenience foods and some disposables, such as paper napkins instead of cloth ones. Still, you can recycle the usual bottles, cans, and paper. You might use online sources rather than shopping that takes you all over town. Further, you can help your parents and other second-half-of-lifers learn how to use technology that will spare their energy.

For those in the second half of life

You may be nearing the end of the life stage during which you feed, clothe, and cart kids around. You are probably moving out of the accumulating phase of life and are able to let go of extra stuff around the house. You may also have a bit more discretionary time. This can free you to take recycling to the next level of precycling (reducing what you buy) or to research the complicated decisions about what is the most energy-efficient appliance or car. You may even be at a point where you have the freedom to consider downsizing to a smaller home or moving closer to your workplace and other locations important to you. This is a time to be grateful that you've made it this far.

Waste Less Stuff

Most conscientious people are familiar with the ecology mantra of reduce, reuse, recycle. Recycling is what most people think of as the "green movement," and certainly recycling bottles, cans, and paper is good to do. Recycling clothes and household goods, however, is different from putting them out in a curbside recycling bin. It took effort to figure out where to take my giveaways. Organizations such as Goodwill, St. Vincent de Paul, thrift stores, and other charities were my first thoughts. I discovered that my geographic area also has services such as Viet Vets and the Lupus Foundation, which have trucks that come through neighborhoods periodically to pick up used goods. Online services, such as the Freecycle Network (www.freecycle.org), offered more ways for getting stuff I no longer needed to people who could use it. (See appendix for a list of national resources.)

Still, there were specialized items such as electronics and tarnished silver that I was happy to give free to a good home, if only I knew which home needed it. There were also weird or useless items—old VCR tapes, political campaign buttons, and vinyl record albums—that took time and creativity to pass along. I asked friends, found a few local resources, and repurposed a few things. I wanted to avoid just adding to a landfill somewhere if there was some use for these items, but it was hard. The electronics I usually took to local office supply stores that recycle them responsibly. I polished the silver and took it to an upscale consignment shop whose proceeds go to support cancer patients. I hung a few of our kids' old shiny game CDs in my garden to scare off deer. (This was semisuccessful.) I also held a yard sale for the neighborhood in which everything was free. You can take the quick and easy way and just take your stuff to a secondhand store, or take the time and effort to find just the right recipient. I did some of both, although it's much more satisfying to match the giveaway to a person who needs it.

Of course the best way to recycle is to reduce the need for it by buying and accumulating less in the first place. This is sometimes called precycling. It is the heart of the simple lifestyle or minimalist movement. If you're still struggling to tame how much comes into your home, revisit chapter 4, "Consume Less—Save More Money." (See appendix for other precycling resources.)

The other end of precycling is to reuse items, which often means repairing them. Now this one sometimes takes real effort, time, skill, and tools. For the handy and crafty, it's a natural solution and can even be fun. Sometimes it works for me. (I'm a big fan of duct tape and super glue.) But other times I have to let go of the ideal in order to get beyond ground zero. Let's face it; I'm never going to know what to do with all those miscellaneous computer parts. Besides, most of them are obsolete by now. The best I can do is dispose of them responsibly.

Waste Less Energy

I vacillate between picking up the car keys or riding my bike to the post office. It's only a few blocks away, but most of the time I'm in a hurry. The dilemma is that wasted energy comes in at least two forms: fossil fuels and human. Driving our car less saves on polluting carbon emissions. Walking or riding my bike can rectify this (plus it's healthy) but it does take time, thus wasting human energy. Of course I might trade the bike ride to the post office for time spent doing indoor exercises or working out in a gym, thus making it a zero sum game. Again, it can become very complicated to figure out the best way to make the most use of my time while saving the earth.

The fossil fuels that run our cars and heat and cool our homes are probably the biggest source of energy waste for most Americans. Electrical appliances follow close behind. Do we have to make trade-offs between using human energy or fossil fuels? Sometimes yes, but we can begin to wean ourselves off wasteful energy and, with the help of science and government, substitute cleaner, more long-lasting power solutions.

For example, once our kids were sprung and both Jim and I started working from home, we downsized to one car. That wouldn't work for everyone, but it works for us. Then our almost 200,000-mile reliable Toyota died. We were sad, but it was an opportunity. Perhaps now was the time that used hybrids had come down in price enough that we could afford one. They had, and we bought one. We do the usual things that most energy-conscious people do, such as wear sweaters in the winter and not much in the summer. Still, I find that I'm not a very productive worker when it gets too hot and humid. So, do I waste electrical energy on air conditioning or human energy through sluggishness?

These are tough calls. The goal is to take a step and then decide mindfully what will move me in a less wasteful direction. It's often a matter of weighing convenience versus environmental impact. If I can just put on an extra layer to keep warm in the winter, fine. No big deal. But there's only so much I can take off in the summer. We have a couple of room air conditioners for the worst heat days. Personally, my solution is simply to go to my basement office to cool off during the hottest part of the day. Others may choose to reconfigure some of your household space to take advantage of the changing seasons. In extreme weather, hot or cold, you may shut off some rooms so that you don't have to cool or heat them. On hot days, maybe you grill outside or serve foods that don't require cooking rather than heat up the kitchen. Some people shift around their homes according to natural lighting—using rooms that are well-lit naturally during the day and thus cutting down on artificial lighting.

It gets a little harder when the energy that's being wasted is my own. I hate to waste time whether it be on hold with tech support or in a line of traffic a mile from home. Having a smart phone could save me some time while waiting at the doctor's office, although I could just take a book. Having a GPS certainly saves me time from being lost. Multitasking—reading the paper while eating or listening to the news while exercising—seems virtuous to me. But do I want to multitask at the expense of mindfulness and focus? Constantly being busy incurs its own cost. Sometimes we humans just need down time—quiet time to relax and let the empty space be filled with daydreams or God. Sometimes these are the same. Remember that God often visited humans in dreams whether day or night. We each have to evaluate which forms of technology save us time, energy, and money—while also recognizing when the technology clutters life. Saving time to consult with God has helped me see my way through the muddle.

Create Less Garbage

It's common sense not to waste our possessions or energy, but garbage *is* waste, so what's the problem with throwing it out? The problem is that the garbage I put out weekly for the garbage collector doesn't just go away. It goes to landfills which hang around for a long time. Beyond my lifetime and the lifetime of my children's children, my garbage can pollute God's creation. I can't believe that this was God's intention when saying to humankind, "Be fruitful and multiply, and fill the earth and subdue it; and have dominion over the fish of the sea and over the birds of the air and over every living thing that moves upon the earth" (Genesis 1:28). I don't think God was imagining landfills.

Concern for the integrity of creation is what led me to my latest Lenten practice: A Waste-Less Lent. I wanted to lessen my carbon footprint by recycling and precycling more. I figured that this heightened awareness of what is garbage and what is not, might help me clean out my soul of wasteful words and malicious thoughts.

I thought I knew a lot about what was recyclable. After all, we have a pretty comprehensive curbside recycling program in my city, and we've been recycling bottles, cans, and paper for years. We also take batteries, electronics, and plastic bags to their respective recycling centers. Jim commented that we should qualify for a carbon offset considering all the recyclables we pick up on our daily walk. But now I was getting really serious. After all, this was Lent, and I wanted to do more.

What counts as garbage? I decided *not* to count:

- Anything that I would recycle (paper, plastic bags, plastic containers, glass, cans)
- Anything that goes into the compost pile or down the disposal

- Anything that goes down the toilet

I did count:

- Anything that I would normally put in the weekly garbage collection

The hardest part of this experiment was the grocery shopping because I had to research whether I could recycle things like milk cartons (yes) and frozen orange juice containers (no). I discovered a TerraCycling center in our area, and thus learned what "TerraCycling" means. Basically, it's a recycling service that takes items that traditional recycling doesn't accept, such as plastic drink cups, snack bags, and candy wrappers. Schools and churches that collect TerraCycle objects can turn them in for money, and thus it becomes a fundraiser (see appendix). I learned that dryer lint is compostable but that dryer sheets are neither compostable nor recyclable. In the end, I didn't achieve zero waste but I did get six weeks of garbage to fit into one trash can. It was a messy project, but so is life. Since most of what I learned about recycling is dependent upon local municipality policies, your research will consist of contacting your city or county public works department. You might begin by typing into your favorite search engine: "Can I recycle _____?"

But wait! It's one thing to reduce what goes into your garbage can; it's another to dispose of it responsibly. I learned that certain things, like batteries, light bulbs, motor oil, pesticides, paints, tires, chemicals, electronics, mercury, prescription medicines, and aerosol cans, needn't be relegated to a landfill but do need to be taken to specialized places. Often cities have annual household hazardous waste days. I've yet to find anyone who takes Styrofoam. Best to precycle it by not using it in the first place.

Through the whole process of trying to waste less stuff, energy, and garbage, there were several principles that emerged worthy of contemplation.

- We are creatures of convenience. In the absence of increased awareness, most of us will choose convenience over ecology or frugality. It's easier to throw the pop can in the trash than to put it into a recycling container—unless the recycling bin is as convenient as the regular trash can. It's more convenient to buy processed food than to buy fresh foods or organic, which are often more expensive. Our culture has trumped frugality with convenience, but it wasn't always that way. We can change. We can make reusing and recycling convenient.

- Cultivate habits, routines, and systems. When Jim and I first switched to taking reusable bags for our shopping, it was a conscious decision. With repetition, it became a habit and automatic. When we first started to pick up trash during our daily walk, we had to remember to take a bag and then also remember to watch for recyclables. Now, it feels unnatural to walk by a plastic bottle without picking it up. Since we have a regular place and system for collecting recyclables and know where to take them, this has become easy. The hard part was the first step and setting up the system. It's like the first time you take a bus, train, or plane to a new location. You may feel a little nervous or awkward the first time, but with repetition it becomes easier and even mindless.

First Steps and Big Steps

Light and easy

Try to fast from using any electricity for a day. This is mostly a consciousness-raising experience and could be fun, especially with kids. An alternative would be to watch your garbage for a day. Again, you're not doing anything extra, just paying attention to what you throw in the trash. It's a preparatory step.

Take a next step by finding out what your city recycles. If your town provides curbside recycling, great! If not, repurpose or purchase a container or two for basic recyclables. Resolve to at least recycle paper, bottles, and cans. If you're already doing this, then you can graduate to finding one or two charities in your locale you can give your used but usable household items to. (See appendix for ideas.) If you're already doing this too, congratulations! Now you can advance to the "Even Greener Club" and research where to take those items that need specialized care such as electronics and household hazardous waste. Take at least one hard-to-recycle item to your newly found resource and spread the word to your neighbors.

Extreme lightness

Presuming that you already recycle most things and have reduced your household trash to a minimum, you can move on to consider your car. (If you are already car-free, you can proceed straight to green heaven—unless you fly a lot, in which case, hopefully you're using carbon credits offered by companies and governments to offset the greenhouse gas emissions from air travel.) Can you reduce the number of cars your family has by one? If this is not practical, consider the kind of car you have. If it is not already a hybrid or electric, could your next car be one? While you're waiting, drive less.

Consider your home. Research how you can reduce energy use. Are solar panels or replacement windows possible? It's an expense, but eventually you recoup the cost through heating/cooling savings. Perhaps it's time to downsize to a smaller home that requires less energy—both fossil fuel and human.

For Meditation

And God said, "Let the waters under the sky be gathered together into one place, and let the dry land appear."

And it was so. God called the dry land Earth, and the waters that were gathered together he called Seas. And God saw that it was good. Then God said, "Let the earth put forth vegetation: plants yielding seed, and fruit trees of every kind on earth that bear fruit with the seed in it." And it was so. The earth brought forth vegetation: plants yielding seed of every kind, and trees of every kind bearing fruit with the seed in it. And God saw that it was good. And there was evening and there was morning, the third day.

And God said, "Let there be lights in the dome of the sky to separate the day from the night; and let them be for signs and for seasons and for days and years, and let there be lights in the dome of the sky to give light upon the earth." And it was so. God made the two great lights—the greater light to rule the day and the lesser light to rule the night—and the stars. God set them in the dome of the sky to give light upon the earth, to rule over the day and over the night, and to separate the light from the darkness. And God saw that it was good. And there was evening and there was morning, the fourth day.

And God said, "Let the waters bring forth swarms of living creatures, and let birds fly above the earth across the dome of the sky." So God created the great sea monsters and every living creature that moves, of every kind, with which the waters swarm, and every winged bird of every kind. And God saw that it was good. God blessed them, saying, "Be fruitful and multiply and fill the waters in the seas, and let birds multiply on the earth." And there was evening and there was morning, the fifth day.

And God said, "Let the earth bring forth living creatures of every kind: cattle and creeping things and wild animals of the earth of every kind." And it was so. God made the wild animals of the earth of every kind, and the cattle of every kind, and everything that creeps upon the ground of every kind. And God saw that it was good.

—Genesis 1:9–25

For Reflection or Discussion

- Just for fun, consider the six "days" of creation and pick one to omit. How would this impact the rest of the environmental balance?

- What things do I normally recycle? What could be a next step for me?

- Where do I generally take clothes, household items, or electronics that I no longer need? Do I need a plan or do I have resources to share?

- How do I decide when to save money or when to go for convenience instead? How do I decide when to act according to my concern for the environment and when to do what is more convenient or expedient?

10

Hurry and Worry Less—Smile and Laugh More

I worry about my health, our kids, our world, whether people will like me, and whether my favorite Survivor player will be voted off the island.

I calculate the quickest route to the grocery, work, and church. I take shortcuts whenever possible and feel impatient with long-winded speakers. I multitask whenever possible: folding laundry while watching a show, listening to a webinar while checking e-mail, making phone calls while a passenger on a trip.

I'm a type A personality and often in a hurry, trying to do lots of things and do them fast. Instead of exercising the self-discipline to prioritize my work, I just try to do it all more quickly. Then I remember what Courtney Carver says in her *Be More with Less* blog, "Say No, so you can say Yes." This helps tame my guilt and focus on what is most important.

But I do want to be responsible and prove that I'm a good enough person. When I *can* slow down enough to be thoughtful, I can usually talk myself out of the self-defeating notion that my worth depends on how much I do or on another's opinion of me. Still, the negative emotions of worry, anger, fear, sadness, guilt, as well as compulsions can weigh me down. I know I'm not alone, because other people tell me their similar sagas.

Perhaps you're the opposite. Perhaps you naturally lean toward optimism and a laissez-faire style of life. Good, let's get together and balance each other out! I'm sure I can give you a few things to worry and stress about. You do want to be more responsible and reliable, don't you?

The more I decluttered my life physically, the more I paid attention to what really provided joy and meaning. I had begun all of this as a Lenten practice, thinking it would somehow deepen my relationship with God, but I assumed that would happen primarily by my doing good works. What I found through my Sunday breaks (days when I didn't give anything away but pondered the meaning of it all) was that there were also emotions that I needed to let go of. This resulted in my personal recovery program. It's based on letting go of the notion that I am the center of the universe and that I can lose God's love. It's helped to take myself less seriously, to lighten up, and to apply **Rule of Thumb #9: Smile and laugh more**.

Connecting to Your Stage of Life
For those in the first half of life

Some of our young adult children are worry warriors and some are relaxed procrastinators. Regardless, I fervently love them all "just the way [they] are." (Remember Mr. Rogers?) There is plenty for young adults to worry about. Will I be able to succeed in my profession? Will I find a loving spouse? Will our kids turn out okay? Will the environment collapse before I do? Some folk become alcoholics, workaholics, or worry-aholics trying to cope with changing times and negative emotions. Dealing with negative emotions transcends chronological age. What self-defeating emotions do *you* need to let go of?

For those in the second half of life

For us elders, we may have overcome the worries of our younger years about career, marriage, and parenting—or maybe not. You still may be paying for college, and worrying about our kids is a never-ending part of parenthood. Still, new worries and fears about health and the limitations of aging may loom.

Taming Time

Letting go of time is counterintuitive for me because I'm very much an efficient, multitasking, time-conscious person. This is why it has been a spiritual challenge to break out of my time-obsessed way of doing things. During my year of daily giveaways, I made it a point to rest on Sundays. That Sabbath time became important not only to attend church but also to reflect on the meaning of stuff in my life, and to curb any pride that might be creeping into my efforts.

Eventually I was led to appreciate that probably the hardest thing for me to give away was time itself. I had to strip myself of working too much and make room for some open space in my day. Eventually, I also became more in tune with the claim that others have on my time as increased opportunities for hospitality came my way. Here are some ways in which letting go of my time turned into blessing.

Personal time

Jesus spent time in the desert and went off to pray in lonely places. Even though I'm not a morning person, I became more "religious" about honoring some private time for prayer at the beginning of my day. Much of it is just sitting in silence and listening to myself, to nature, to God speaking through thoughts and Scripture.

Time to welcome others

Whether it was a graced message or just coincidence, who knows, but during my time of diligently giving stuff away, a number of opportunities to host travelers or others in need came our way. Since our kids are sprung, we have three extra bedrooms. If we were not going to downsize our house, it seemed only right to share the space with others. Some stayed longer than expected but all brought fullness to our life. It did take time to clean, wash sheets, and feed more people, but often they fed us with interesting international dishes, music, and stimulating conversation.

Volunteer time

Reducing our lifestyle expectations meant that we didn't need as much income to survive, especially after the kids moved out. Thus, neither my husband nor I are employed full time. This is good. We have enough money to get by but, more important, we have time to say yes to volunteer projects, boards, and groups. The challenge for us has been to know when to say no. It's flattering to be asked to lead an organization or chair a worthy cause, but not at the price of being a cranky leader or a stressed spouse. How do we know when to say no? I ask those closest to me and take it to God in prayer.

Saved time

Volumes have been written about saving time. In addition to the basics of prioritizing, delegating, and multitasking, our kids have recently been showing us the advantages of online shopping. Since several of our children live overseas, they order Christmas presents delivered straight to our house. I recently went to six neighborhood stores looking for some simple mittens and found none. When I got home, I realized I could have saved time and money by purchasing them online. Of course, my conscience then pipes up and says, "Remember the toll this can take on local merchants who can't compete with the big box or online stores. Remember the toll on the environment that shipping goods all over the world can take?" Less buying in general can save time and pangs of conscience.

Emotional Baggage

Some of our heaviest burdens are the ones we carry in our hearts and minds. This is why we need reminders such as **Rule of Thumb #8: Let go of anger, grudges, and compulsions to lighten the heart**.

Worry

Letting go of worries has helped me distinguish between productive and nonproductive worries. Tomorrow's bad weather is something I can't control. Worrying will not change it. I might make some contingency plans if it's possible and important, but otherwise, I push it out of my mind. Whether a health test will come back positive or negative cannot be changed by my worry. Praying and sharing my concern with those who love me can be comforting until I know the actual results. Beyond that, I need to resist the worry and put it aside.

But pushing worries out of my consciousness is easier said than done. Letting go often requires substituting another thought or activity whenever the worry returns. As a person of faith, I have been helped by vigilantly returning to prayer at such times. Although I am generally not fond of repetitive or memorized prayers, for really stubborn worries, the rosary has helped me. Sometimes I just don't have the creative energy to come up with a spontaneous prayer. When I was worried about whether I would need some of the things I gave away, it helped to know that others needed them more. When worried about money or health, it helped my perspective to spend time with those who had struggles of their own.

Anger

The target of my anger can be as personal as an individual whom I find difficult to deal with or as broad as my country (think politics and greed), my Church (think scandals and failure to love unconditionally), or the world (think environmental degradation, wars, and poverty). I could go on, but that just makes me madder. So how do I let go of my anger? Generally, I bring it to prayer. The complaints come unbidden, so I might as well integrate it into prayer. What I've found helpful is to balance anger with gratitude. Near the end of my daily give-away year, I decided to intentionally note one thing each day that I was grateful for and to do this during morning prayer. I call this my "gratitude offensive."

It's been a good experience for me. As soon as I start fretting about the ills of our society, I call to mind that at least I have electricity and running water, or that we finally decided on which car to buy and had the money to buy it, or that my back pain and cold left in time for me to enjoy a dance weekend, or that there's a gentle breeze today, or . . .

If it's a person I feel angry toward, I've taken it to confession and forced myself to think of a positive quality that person possesses and then hold him or her in prayer. This may take a lot of repetition. I keep reminding myself: Don't quibble over small stuff; let it go, and substitute gratitude. Remember **Rule of Thumb #10, Part 1: Forgive others. It will lift your spirit**.

Sadness

Sadness, whether serious like a death or relatively minor like the loss of a favorite memento, is an emotion that can't be hurried. Take the time to feel it. Don't squelch it; it will pass eventually. The "letting go" may be a matter of letting go of *your* timing.

There are some mistakes I've made that I regret and that our children keep reminding me of in humorous ways. I no longer feel sad about them but have had to forgive myself for being human. Remember **Rule of Thumb #10, Part 2: Forgive yourself. It will lift your spirit**.

Fear

Fear and worry are related emotions, although fear generally has a more realistic source and thus can be harder to let go of. One of the guests who stayed with us while trying to get her family back together eventually moved on. This was good. Knowing her financial need and a history of stealing when she was a juvenile, however, I found myself fearful. She returned our house key, but I started wondering if she might have made a copy. I didn't think so and I wanted to trust, but the fear remained. I wasn't sure if it was prudence or lack of trust to change our locks. I bought new locks, and our keys have been fussy ever since. The locksmith doesn't return my calls. Who knows whether this is a message that my trust was too weak or if it's just coincidence. Don't let fear immobilize you from doing good. Trust in God but verify with humans.

Guilt

Conscientious people are likely candidates for giving generously to others. Conscientious people can also be prone to guilt. At the end of my year of giving away, I felt good until I looked around our home and didn't notice an appreciable difference. Sure, some shelves were clear of clutter, my closet was a little leaner, and the space under our bed and other remote hiding places was now freer, but I still had more possessions than I needed. I felt a little guilty that I was so public about giving stuff away but that it had been relatively painless for me.

I also periodically feel guilty about mistakes I've made in parenting, about my failure to stand up for my beliefs, or not spending enough time with my aging parents. I decided to make a list of the biggest mistakes I've made and save it on my computer. This has been freeing because I don't have to keep reminding myself of them. I know I can always just look them up if I need a dose of humility. Mostly I repeat the mantra, "I did the best I could with what I knew at the time. I cannot change the past; I can only try to do better in the future."

Compulsions

Some people are compulsive shoppers, eaters, or counters. If you've read this far in my book, you recognize some of my compulsions: getting a bargain, organizing, and making things compact. Letting go of a compulsion can be a difficult habit to break. If it's not hurting you or anybody else, maybe you can just continue organizing all the Legos in the house as I did one weekend when I wanted a mindless way to pass some time. If the compulsion is bothering you or others, substitute other more desirable activities and ask for help.

Lighten Up Your Attitude

In addition to substituting gratitude, prayer, and worthy works when troublesome emotions accost us, I've found another strategy that can pull me out of a funk: humor. I am not by nature very funny or humorous, but I'm learning from others.

One of my best lessons was when I received a box in the mail from an unknown "fan." He said he had been following my blog about giving things away and figured I would know the best way to dispose of his collectibles. It sounded a little fishy, but I gave the mystery giver the benefit of the doubt. The box included Styrofoam cups, forty-five pieces of scrap paper, a match, earplugs, a pair of broken sunglasses, some golf pencils, a zipper, a half bag of seeds, a plastic doll, a self-esteem cassette tape, an empty egg carton, plus more. Hmmm. I spent the next thirty minutes sleuthing on the Internet to figure out who my secret admirer was. Based on the postmark I guessed it was a friend and colleague who lives in New Haven, Connecticut. I was right and we both had a good laugh. The moral of the story was not to take myself too seriously. Even better was the knowledge that someone spent the time and three dollars to send some laughter my way. Pass it on and make someone laugh today.

Fortunately I'm also married to a person who takes joy in finding ways to trick and fool me. After I figure out the latest place he's hidden the rubber ducky or that the President of the United States didn't actually call to offer me a humanitarian reward for spreading my wealth, we have a good laugh and it lifts my spirits.

When friends aren't around to prompt a laugh, I can always go to my favorite political parody news program on television. A fallback strategy that seems artificial but works nevertheless is to force a smile or a laugh. Repeat till you feel silly. Sometimes doing such an inane thing is funny enough in itself.

First Steps and Big Steps

Light and easy
What's your biggest worry? Exaggerate it. Tell someone else your exaggeration and hear how ridiculous it sounds. Laugh together.

Choose one person who irritates you. Write down one positive quality that person has. Hold that person in prayer for one day.

Extreme lightness
Determine which activity is the biggest unproductive time hog in your life. Substitute a practice that will bring you more fulfillment. It could be opening more space for prayer, committing to play more games with your kids, or getting more exercise.

For those of us who care mightily about fostering a more "environmentally sustainable, socially just, and spiritually fulfilling presence on this earth," it's easy to feel discouraged by our society's lack of progress. Let your discouragement, anger, worry, and fear be a catalyst for action. Check out the Pachamama Alliance's Awakening the Dreamer Symposium as a vehicle for making a difference. (See bibliography.)

For Meditation

Therefore I tell you, do not worry about your life, what you will eat or what you will drink, or about your body, what you will wear. Is not life more than food, and the body more than clothing? Look at the birds of the air; they neither sow nor reap nor gather into barns, and yet your heavenly Father feeds them. Are you not of more value than they? And can any of you by worrying add a single hour to your span of life? And why do you worry about clothing? Consider the lilies of the field, how they grow; they neither toil nor spin, yet I tell you, even Solomon in all his glory was not clothed like one of these. But if God so clothes the grass of the field, which is alive today and tomorrow is thrown into the oven, will he not much more clothe you—you of little faith? Therefore do not worry, saying, "What will we eat?" or "What will we drink?" or "What will we wear?" For it is the Gentiles who strive for all these things; and indeed your heavenly Father knows that you need all these things. But strive first for the kingdom of God and his righteousness, and all these things will be given to you as well. So do not worry about tomorrow, for tomorrow will bring worries of its own. Today's trouble is enough for today.

—Matthew 6:25–34

For Reflection or Discussion

- What's my biggest fear or worry about the future? Can I do something about it, or is it my habit to complain instead?

- On a scale of 1–10, with 1 being "I'm usually in a hurry" and 10 being "I'm usually a pretty laid-back procrastinator," where would I put myself? How could I bring more balance to my use of time?

- Who do I know who is the opposite of me in the areas of hurrying or worrying? What are the pros and cons of both styles?
- Hurrying can rob us of the gift of spending leisure time with others. On whom do I need to lavish some time today?
- What brings joy and contentment to my life? Plan to do one of those things within the next week.
- What makes me laugh?

11

Let Go of Cheap Faith—Gain a Deeper Faith

Sally obeys all the rules, goes to church weekly plus, and tithes. Joe doesn't, but he's kind and tirelessly works for the poor and social justice. Who is holier? Who knows?

The Smug Factor

About halfway through my year of giving stuff away, I was feeling pretty successful and self-satisfied. After all, I was doing good for other people while cleaning out duplicates and nonessentials from my home. Because I was blogging about it, it was a frequent topic of conversation. Others seemed motivated to start or intensify thinning their own possessions. I was feeling pretty happy about my progress. Although I would never say it out loud, I found myself internally disdaining those who lived lives of conspicuous consumption. In short, I felt superior and smug.

Eventually, however, I realized that I'm not the only one pruning my life. Given uncluttered time, space, and prayer, new insights welled up in me. I attribute them to the Divine at work. I started to see how I hung on to pride and felt self-righteous. Sometimes this smugness was punctured by an embarrassing incident, such as the time I challenged the young mother who had just moved from our home to a transitional shelter about her new manicure. Wasn't there something better she should be using her meager funds on? She explained that the shelter had some volunteers who occasionally came to treat the women to manicures. Oops! Whether coincidence or a graced moment, I think of it as the hand of God yanking me out of self-righteousness.

Another time I was trying so hard to give away a baby crib. Our son and daughter-in-law had gently informed us that although they appreciated our hanging on to it for thirty-some years so that our grandchild would have a crib when they visited, did we know that cribs with drop sides had been recalled for safety reasons? We did some research and felt satisfied that the recall did not apply to *our* crib, but it wasn't worth straining family relationships so we searched for other needy recipients. Certainly a maternity home or women's shelter could use it. "Sorry, we can't take that kind of crib either." One person close to me bluntly said, "So you're willing to give a crib to someone else that you wouldn't trust for your own grandchild." Ouch. She was right. Then another friend came up with the clever idea of repurposing the crib as a love seat. Take off the front rail, put some big cushions on the back, and cover the mattress. Perfect! I did it and called Viet Vets to pick up the "couch." When the truck arrived, they politely informed me that they couldn't accept anything with a mattress because of the bed bug potential. I had proudly told many people of the creative plan I had for this crib. I had to eat my words.

So, we used the crib for parts. The mattress goes on the floor for visiting toddlers. I use the rails in our garden for climbing plants. The wood parts went for firewood. The metal parts can be recycled. It took a long time to get to this point. It's humbling. Sometimes it's hard to do good.

The spiritual wisdom I gained was to watch out for self-righteousness. Judging myself as better or more virtuous than others is a trap of superficial faith. Letting go of self-righteousness is probably the biggest challenge for people like me who generously give things away. Humility is sometimes forced upon us by circumstances, but a deeper faith walks with the words of the prophet Micah, "What does the Lord require of you but to do justice, and to love kindness, and to walk humbly with your God?" (Micah 6:8).

This wisdom also urges me to forgive myself for my failures of spirit and of practice. Recognize the self-righteousness, repent, and move on. And do the same for others, especially those who don't seem to be as motivated as I think they should be to declutter or help out! Whether my efforts don't go well, or I struggle with what others do or don't do, I need Rule of Thumb #10: Forgive others. Forgive yourself. It will lift your spirit.

Connecting to Your Stage of Life

For those in the first half of life

We live in a culture of independence and individualism. "Because I said so" is usually not good enough, no matter whether the authority is a parent, a government, or the institutional church. Some yearn for the mysticism, roots, and community that organized religion can offer. Others never experienced these graces or have become disillusioned and search for their meaning in social causes, nature, and humanitarian endeavors—some spiritual, some not. The challenge during this stage of life is not to become jaded and give up. No human institution is perfect. The meaning is in the seeking.

For those in the second half of life

Elders are not immune to disillusionment with the church. With scandals and hypocrisy permeating our culture and religious institutions, it's tempting to hibernate with a few close friends or simply to leave. The challenge is to dig deeper into what our faith is all about. We must grow beyond the faith of our youth (the "pray, pay, and obey" kind of faith) and develop a mature, well informed, and reflective faith that transcends artificial rules in pursuit of the *Why* behind the rules. We've lived long enough to understand that rules made by humans can evolve or have exceptions (such as, asking the father of your fiancée for permission to marry his daughter, or fasting from midnight before Communion, or not eating meat on Fridays).

From the Letter to the Spirit

Faith can be a motivation and a comfort to people throughout life. Even those who are not connected with an organized religion usually want to live in a meaningful way and make a positive difference in our world. I started with letting go of material things because I listened to the biblical Scriptures calling us to be our brother's keeper (Genesis 4:9). Eventually I started to recognize intangible things that I also had to let go of, such as negative emotions and self-righteousness. Giving away material possessions was a way of making psychological space for the deeper attitudinal changes I needed to make.

I had loving parents and many years of Catholic schooling, both of which predisposed me to habits: prayer, examining my conscience, serving the poor and marginalized. As an adult, I built on these through participating in several small faith communities that challenged me to know not just the letter of the law but the spirit behind the rules and customs. I was lucky to find a soul mate who shared my values. Which came first—faith or the impulse to spend my life trying to contribute to the well-being of others? Who knows? One leads to the other. As Franciscan priest and author Richard Rohr reminds us, we must balance action and contemplation. Then we circle around again.

Cheap faith provides a roof over our heads and gets us started, but we are meant to outgrow it. It's like moving from the letter of the law to understanding its spirit. The Ten Commandments are a foundation, but we can get stuck on the letter of the law. We say, "Okay, I didn't kill anybody today, so I'm good." We go to Mass (or whatever your regular worship form is), and say grace before meals. We might even do additional devotional practices, serve on the parish council, chair the annual church festival, or chaperone the teen's overnight church event. These can feel like a penance at times. We might conjecture that they should certainly count for something toward salvation! Don't stop doing these things, but long-haul faith means adding mindfulness and subtracting superstition and empty practices.

As you can imagine, my daily giveaways took some self-discipline. Sometimes I would plan a week ahead for convenience. I got into a lot of counting and measuring. (For example, do I count the 300+ *National Geographics* as one lot or almost a year of giveaways?) During my Waste-Less Lent I was tempted to flush things down the toilet so I didn't need to count it as garbage. Once a disposable cup blew into our yard. I wanted to put it in our neighbor's garbage can since I wasn't sure it could be recycled. I overcame those temptations but I did squish my garbage down in its can so it didn't look like as much when I measured it.

Ultimately I faced several spiritual issues:

- The Spirit Trumps the Letter: When in doubt about a moral issue, always side with Jesus' compassion. Remember the woman caught in adultery, Jesus healing on the Sabbath, the disciples plucking grain on the Sabbath.

- Attitudes: Let go of the need to be right, to have things my way, and to judge others or even myself. Am I doing this just to look virtuous?

- Self-sacrifice: Give away time and money, not just stuff. Am I willing to give and to act even when it's inconvenient or costs me time or money?

- Self-emptying: Let go of grudges. Is this really helping me to be a more loving person, thus bringing me closer to God; or is it all about me?

Prayer and Religion

How do I know when to use the "Spirit Trumps the Letter" approach to a moral decision and when is it just rationalizing what I want to do? I pray. My own approach to prayer has evolved over the years. Jim and I used to have a daily devotional time. This was good but it took too much planning, and thus we found ourselves avoiding it. During our years with babies, we tried to anticipate their waking time and would get up fifteen minutes earlier for our own prayer time. This didn't always work. We figured God was speaking through our child's need and let the formal prayer go. After much experimentation we eventually settled on a brief morning offering and then silent listening through spiritual reading or just being quiet, perhaps doing some journaling.

This type of prayer is most often how I seek to sort out the letter of the law from the spirit of the law. Fewer words make space for quiet listening. Some people pray through meditation, some say memorized prayers, some absorb the wonder of creation and see that "It is good." Some look at that same creation and are frightened by the power of wind, rain, and fire, wondering about the source of such a destructive force. Finding God in all things is the core of Ignatian spirituality but it can be a challenge and a mystery. Some things look very mundane and ordinary; hardly holy looking. Others look fearsome and confusing. It's both daunting and awesome. That's why we need to let go of cheap faith and deepen our faith for the long haul.

I try to recognize God in the traditional ways of worship and then go straight to the source. We talk it over. I figure God came to us in the person of Jesus and continues to touch our lives through the Holy Spirit. I can't prove it, but I choose to believe it. The home I've found for this faith is through the Catholic Church, warts and all. It's not perfect because the institutional church is all of us who participate, and we are not perfect. Yet, I believe we are guided through the Holy Spirit, who comes to us through prayer and the community of believers.

Others have found inspiration through other spiritual paths, and I respect that. We must work together since God is the God of all, no matter what name we give to our divine encounters.

But faith is not solely a private affair. Communal worship is a source of human strength and discernment. The Spirit speaks when we observe the faith of others and when we talk with them about hard topics and difficult decisions. Sometimes I believe that God sends messages through other people and they don't always have wings.

The Long Haul: Aging, Death, and Beyond

Age is a funny thing. I usually feel pretty young, except when I don't. Although I walk, camp, dance, and do a lot of other physical things, I definitely do not do heavy lifting. I'm aware that I can no longer swoop toddlers up in my arms and put them in a crib or other places they would rather not go. I watch my parents, who are still living independently but need increasing help, and I see in them my future self—if I am blessed to live that long. Letting go of physical limitations is scary enough. Watching beloved elders deal with decreasing memory is daunting. These days I ask Jim each time I can't remember a name or a word whether I'm losing it. He usually replies that he can't remember what I asked.

Holy Week at the end of Lent is a reminder that life moves from the glory of Palm Sunday and the community of the Last Supper to the suffering of the crucifixion, and ultimately to the Resurrection. One of my most inspired giveaways happened on Holy Thursday when I took a supper to Birdie. Birdie was my Kris Kringle partner at our parish the previous Advent. I never met her but prayed for her and sent her a card. From our parish directory I knew that she was African American. Jim and I had been trying to get to know more people in our parish, especially people of other races. We have a racially diverse parish but often people don't mix. We decided to invite Birdie over for dinner, but she had been ill and had not been able to come. I decided to make a lasagna dinner for Birdie and take it to her. Since Holy Thursday commemorates the Last Supper, I chose that day. We talked about life, illness, and her diminishing ability to get from her home to church. Even though I'm not a great cook we had a great evening. Fortunately, it wasn't her "last supper," and I continued to look for her at church.

For the past few years, the focus of Holy Week has become more personal as I identify with the uncertainty of how my life will eventually end. I don't dwell on this much but I know it is inevitable. I am blessed to have the example of parents who are accepting their own limitations with grace and humor. I don't expect to die soon, but who knows when "soon" will be. As I give things away, I become more aware that I can't take this or that item with me to the next life. In fact, I don't even need it so much for this life. It's a strangely comforting peace to be letting go of stuff gradually in preparation for the final letting go.

First Steps and Big Steps

Light and easy

To recognize your biases and to help fight the smug factor, identify a strongly held belief that you know is controversial (a political candidate or a cause such as abortion, gun control, the environment, or homosexuality). Force yourself to write out a defense of the other side's position. You don't have to agree with it, just make sure it is balanced and that you really try to understand what drives the other side. Have someone else read both sides of the argument to check your potential bias. If you feel like taking a next step, try having a live conversation with someone who holds a different belief from you. Again, the goal is not agreement, but respectful understanding.

Extreme lightness

Where are the blind spots in your own spirituality? Usually we don't recognize these without help from a spouse, child, trusted friend, enemy, or spiritual director. What are you most proud of in your life? This can be a catch-22, since the very thing we're proud of might be the source of self-righteousness. Claiming humility as your item of pride won't work.

For Meditation

If I give away all my possessions, and if I hand over my body so that I may boast, but do not have love, I gain nothing.

—1 Corinthians 13:3

When I was a child, I spoke like a child, I thought like a child, I reasoned like a child; when I became an adult, I put an end to childish ways. For now we see in a mirror, dimly, but then we will see face to face. Now I know only in part; then I will know fully, even as I have been fully known. And now faith, hope, and love abide, these three; and the greatest of these is love.

—1 Corinthians 13:11–13

For Reflection or Discussion

- Have I ever made a difficult decision of conscience? What process did I go through?
- What form does prayer take in my life? Am I satisfied with it? Do I need to change anything or spend more time connecting with God?
- Do I think that I'm smart enough, successful enough, remember enough? Can I accept my limitations?
- Does the idea of my death scare me? How do my thoughts of death influence how I live day by day?

12

What Difference Does It Make?

Giving things away is more than a housecleaning technique, although it does serve that purpose also. After cultivating a habit of looking for things to give away, you may find that you look at shopping differently. You may find that you can't break the habit and continue to see things to give away. You may find that your attitude toward your possessions becomes more generous, or that there are many intangible things that are hard to let go of, such as time and idiosyncrasies. In the end you may figure out how much is enough and how much is too much. My guess is that, like me, you will continue that discernment as the years go by and life goes through its various changes.

As I continue to strip away the unnecessary stuff in my closets and mind, I've been able to see more clearly how much is enough and how much is more than enough. It's a delicate dance to balance my genuine needs with those of others. The spiritual paradox is that the less tightly I hold on to my stuff, my way, and my concerns, the happier I become.

Vexing Questions and Decisions

Still, as I contemplated the dilemma of how to be generous yet responsible and kind but not foolish while trying to live lightly on planet earth, some vexing questions remained:

- Is it immoral to be part of the 1 percent of the richest Americans? Is it my job to judge another's wealth?

- Where do I personally draw the line between "enough" and "more than enough"?

- Maybe I'm not attached to my possessions but hold tight to my opinions and having things my way. Am I so caught up in being right that I'm weighed down by self-righteousness and lose sight of the most important values in life—loving relationships and a deeper spirituality?

Living more lightly can sound wonderfully idealistic but not very practical. When it comes to everyday life, we humans can tie ourselves up in knots trying to figure out how to best live in this complicated world. For example:

- I deliberate over buying the cheaper brand or paying more for organic. Will my thrifty (some would say cheapskate) side win or my health-conscious (green) side?

- I dither over throwing away the soiled blouse or washing it and mending it. If the stain doesn't come out, how many rags does a household really need? And is it proper to give substandard stuff to Goodwill?

- Should I give away that favorite suit that's a bit dated or a little snug, or wait till it comes back into style or I lose a few pounds?

I want to be a conscientious human being, to live lightly upon our earth, and not use any more resources than necessary; but I also want to save time and money. Living simply is not always simple. To keep life from being consumed by tedious, everyday decisions which feel more like a burden than a way to lighten my spirit, try to keep the long haul in mind.

Suggestions for the Long Haul

Take one step, even if it's a baby step

About fifteen years ago, a friend told me she took cloth bags into stores in order to reduce the number of plastic bags she brought home. This sounded admirable and easy enough. I put a cloth bag in our car—and forgot about it till I was in the checkout line. Let go of feeling that you are failing to save the world. Replace the angst or guilt by taking a step, even if it's a baby step. After a few months, I finally started to remember to take the bag into the store with me, some of the time. That's progress. For some people, this will be enough considering all the other responsibilities and pressures you have in your life. Focus on the **Light and easy steps** at the end of each chapter.

Turn a step into a habit

Eventually muscle memory took over, and I'd remember to take a bag (or several bags when grocery shopping) into stores 90 percent of the time. Before my give-away Lent, I occasionally took items to Goodwill but it was a trek and inconvenient. Once I developed a habit of giving things away, I also started noticing where to take these extra items. Some friends tell me they cart their items to St. Vincent de Paul once a month. I get a monthly call from Viet Vets asking if I have anything to donate. It's so much easier to have a system or a routine.

Then I started thinking about other things that I do regularly and how it simplifies my life to build healthy habits into my lifestyle. There's wisdom in the rhythm of going to religious services once a week, the same day every week. Jim and I have a weekly date. It nourishes our marriage. We go to a weekly contra dance. We used to have weekly Family Nights. All these things help our good intentions turn into habits, because anything that we repeat often enough on a regular basis can become automatic.

Participate in systemic change

But will my relatively puny reduction in plastic bags by using cloth bags make any significant reduction in the hole in the ozone layer? Will my recycling bottles and cans reduce carbon emissions enough to make a difference? No, it won't be enough in itself.

But I've found that making these relatively minor changes in my lifestyle changes *me*. It raises my consciousness about the bigger picture. It leads me to think about systemic change that *will* make a difference. These systemic changes almost always involve working with other people, organizations, and the government. This is hard work. It takes team work.

As my friends learn about steps I take, it's quite possible that some of them will be inspired to take similar steps; thus the multiplier effect kicks in. The bigger challenge is for one person's change to influence the broader society. Only when a critical mass of people put pressure on organizations, corporations, and governments, will the culture of acquisition change. This is a bigger task than most people care to take on. That's okay. Do what you can, given your skills and stage of life; then let go of any residual guilt.

The world needs some of us, however, to get involved in systemic change. This level of involvement can create a climate in which others can choose freely to live more simply, knowing that there is a basic safety net when unexpected crises loom. A job loss, health emergency, natural disaster, or war can sabotage the most altruistic person's resources. Some of us must take the step to leverage individual change into institutional change because we care about one another's well-being. It's not easy and it takes time. The slow pace and setbacks can be discouraging. That's why it takes spiritual maturity and community to carry this out over the long haul.

Stay spiritually centered

My Catholic faith and the small faith community with whom I meet regularly help me stay centered and balanced. The rhythms of the liturgical seasons of waiting, rejoicing, sacrificing, praise, and then the long season of ordinary time helps me remember that life is cyclical with ups and downs, joys and heartaches. My community helps me discern when I am overreacting and need to calm down, but also when I should take risks and be courageous. It confirms what I hear in prayer and challenges and supports me to go deeper. We pray together but then go out to turn those prayers into service. The trials of service then drive us back to prayer.

You may have a different spiritual home. The principles, however, are universal. Listen to the Spirit of the God in you. Listen to the Spirit of the Divine in other people. Then act.

My hope is that you become a human lighthouse, a person who has examined his or her home and soul and learned that hanging on to less stuff makes room for the more important stuff. Contributing to the well-being of others usually has the happy side effect of increasing your own happiness and inner peace. Your inner light can be contagious and provide a directional beacon for others. While still on the journey, however, don't be discouraged when you may still face vexing questions and decisions. That is to be expected. You're not home yet.

Bibliography and Suggested Resources

Books

Babauta, Leo. *The Power of Less: The Fine Art of Limiting Yourself to the Essential . . . in Business and in Life*. New York: Hyperion, 2009.

Becker, Joshua. *Living With Less: An Unexpected Key to Happiness (Simply for Students)*. Loveland, CO: Group Publishing Inc., 2012.

Carver, Courtney. *Living in the Land of Enough*. Self published, 2011.

Carver, Courtney. *Simple Ways to Be More with Less*. Self published, 2011.

Corbett, Steve and Brian Fikkert. *When Helping Hurts: How to Alleviate Poverty Without Hurting the Poor . . . and Yourself*. Chicago: Moody Publishers, 2012.

Jay, Francine. *The Joy of Less, A Minimalist Living Guide: How to Declutter, Organize, and Simplify Your Life*. Medford, NJ: Anja Press, 2010.

Leonard, Annie, *The Story of Stuff*. New York: Free Press, 2010.

Millburn, Joshua Fields and Ryan Nicodemus. *Simplicity: Essays*. Missoula, MT: Asymmetrical Press, 2012.

Page, Gretchen Rubin. *The Happiness Project*. New York: Harper Perennial, 2011.

Ramsey, Dave. *The Total Money Makeover: A Proven Plan for Financial Fitness*. Nashville, TN: Thomas Nelson, 2009.

Rosenberg, Marshall B. *Practical Spirituality*. Encinitas, CA: Puddledancer Press, 2004.

Rosenberg, Marshall B. *Nonviolent Communication: A Language of Life*. Encinitas, CA: Puddledancer Press, 2003.

Salwen, Hannah and Kevin Salwen. *The Power of Half: One Family's Decision to Stop Taking and Start Giving Back*. New York: Mariner Books, 2011.

Strobel, Tammy, *You Can Buy Happiness (and It's Cheap): How One Woman Radically Simplified Her Life and How You Can Too*. Novato, CA: New World Library, 2012.

Thoreau, Henry David. *Walden*. USA: Empire Books, 2013.

Turkle, Sherry. *Alone Together: Why We Expect More from Technology and Less from Each Other*. New York: Basic Books, 2012.

Resources

Blogs, Web sites, Programs

The Afflluenza Project. http://www.theaffluenzaproject.com/
http://www.youtube.com/watch?v=QkiR_q-thjg

Awakening the Dreamer. A symposium based on creating a human presence on earth that is environmentally sustainable, socially just, and spiritually fulfilling. 4,000 leaders worldwide facilitate this program. *http://awakenthedreamer.com/*. Sponsored by the Pachamama Alliance *http://www.pachamama.org/*

Becoming Minimalist: How to Live with Less Stuff. Blog by Joshua Becker, *http://www.becomingminimalist.com/how-to-live-with-less/*

Be More With Less. Blog by Courtney Carver, *http://bemorewithless.com/*

Catholics Spending and Acting Justly: A Small-Group Guide for Living Economic Stewardship, Charles K. Wilber. Notre Dame, IN: Ave Maria Press, 2011.

Christian Simplicity: A Gospel Value. A Seven-Session Discussion Course. Passionist Earth and Spirit Center, Louisville, KY, and Passionist Congregation of Holy Cross Province, Chicago, IL, 2011.

A Cluttered Life: Middle-Class Abundance. A six-minute video produced by the University of California. Presents a stunning, visual ethnography that reveals the material culture of today's modern household. *http://www.uctv.tv/shows/ Stuff-A-Cluttered-Life-Middle-Class-Abundance-Ep-1-24699*

Living Lightly. Blog by Susan Vogt on living more simply but abundantly—365 Days of Give-Aways, *http://www.susanvogt.net/ blog*

Next Starfish. Blog by Steve Moreby. Its purpose is to equip and inspire individuals to create positive change in their lives, social networks, organizations, communities, and the world. *http://nextstarfish.com/*

The 333 Project. Blog by Courtney Carver. Project 333 is a fashion challenge that invites you to dress with 33 items or less for 3 months. *http://theproject333.com/*

"What Is Enough Food? 147 Meals Later." Article by Jeff Shinabarger. Jeff asked a bold question, "What if we didn't buy any groceries for the entire month? But lived on all the food in our kitchen pantry, refrigerator and freezer?" *http://www.huffingtonpost.com/jeff-shinabarger/ 147-meals-later_b_2362892.html?utm_hp_ref=tw*

World Vision, Inc. A Christian humanitarian organization dedicated to working with children, families, and their communities worldwide to reach their full potential by tackling the causes of poverty and injustice. *http://www.worldvision.org/*

Have Extra Money or Stuff to Give Away?

Starter List of Where to Donate

It is always more satisfying to give your extra money or possessions to a local cause, ideally one that you are personally connected to. However, since *Blessed by Less* is a book that transcends local boundaries, following is a list of organizations, many of which have local chapters.

American Red Cross. *http://www.redcross.org/*

Catholic Relief Services. *http://crs.org/*

Charity Navigator. America's leading independent charity evaluator, works to advance a more efficient and responsive philanthropic marketplace by evaluating the financial health, accountability, and transparency of 6,000 of America's largest charities. *http://www.charitynavigator.org/*

The FreeCycle Network. A grassroots and entirely nonprofit movement of people who are giving (and getting) stuff for free in their own towns. *http://www.freecycle.org/*

Gazelle. Electronics recycler. *http://www.gazelle.com/*

Goodwill Industries. *http://www.goodwill.org/*

Society of St. Vincent de Paul. *http://www.svdpusa.org/*

A Store Where Everything Is Free. *http://www.greenamerica.org/ livinggreen/freestore.cfm*

United Way. *http://www.unitedway.org/*

Vietnam Veterans of America. *http://www.scheduleapickup.com/*

Where to Get Rid of Anything. *http://www.oprah.com/home/ Where-to-Get-Rid-of-Clothing-Toys-Old-Phones-and-More*

100 Thing Challenge. Dave Bruno reduced his personal possessions to 100 items for a year in order to form new habits of consumption. *http://www.100thingchallenge.com/about-100tc/*

Ecology Resources

Likewise, many of the most practical environmental resources need to be accessed locally. If you are unfamiliar with services near your home, the following resources can get you started.

Awakening the Dreamer. A symposium based on creating a human presence on earth that is environmentally sustainable, socially just, and spiritually fulfilling. 4,000 leaders worldwide facilitate this program. *http://awakenthedreamer.com/.* Sponsored by the Pachamama Alliance *http://www.pachamama.org/*

Citizen's Climate Lobby. http://citizensclimatelobby.org/

Green America. Work for a world where all people have enough, where all communities are healthy and safe, and where the bounty of the earth is preserved for all the generations to come. *http://www.greenamerica.org/about/*

Precycling: Earth911. A comprehensive Web site about precycling and recycling just about everything. *http://earth911.com/news/2012/03/28/precycling-helps-shoppers-save/*

TerraCycling. TerraCycle is a private U.S.small business founded in 2001 and headquartered in Trenton, New Jersey. It specializes in making consumer products from waste materials that are otherwise difficult to recycle. *http://www.terracycle.com/en-US/*

Acknowledgments

Bloggers Courtney Carver, Joshua Becker, Leo Babauta, Joshua Fields Millburn, and many others who regularly inspire readers to keep the values of simple lifestyle, minimalism, and spirituality at the core of their lives.

The hundreds of people who responded to my survey. They described their own efforts to live more lightly and how their faith steers and balances them. Many of these people are members of the National Association of Catholic Family Life Ministers (NACFLM) or readers of my monthly emails, *Marriage Moments* and *Parenting Pointers*. Thank you for your insights.

Guides who have influenced the spirituality undergirding this book are Jesuit James Martin, Franciscan Richard Rohr, the Marianist Family, the Pachamama Alliance, and most fundamentally, the life of Jesus Christ.

About the Author

Susan is a speaker and award-winning author. She has been married for over 40 years to Jim Vogt. They live in Covington, Kentucky, and have four young adult children. For many years, she was the editor of the *Journal of the National Association of Catholic Family Life Ministers* and content editor for the USCCB Web site on marriage. Susan has worked in family ministry for the Catholic Church for over 30 years designing and leading marriage, parenting, and leadership programs. A counselor by training, she has taught on the high school and university level. Susan and her husband have worked with ecumenical and social justice organizations including *Parenting for Peace and Justice*. She has written five books.